Turtles as a Hobby

by W. P. Mara

SAVE-OUR-PLANET SERIES

T.F.H. Publications, Inc.
1 T.F.H. Plaza • Third & Union Aves. • Neptune, NJ 07753

Contents

Inside front and back cover photo credits: (Front) *Deirochelys reticularia.* (Back) *Sternotherus odoratus.* Both photos by Robert T. Zappalorti.

A relative of the popular Reeves's Turtle, *(Chinemys reevesi)*, *Chinemys kwang-tungensis* lives in the mountain streams of Kwangtung, China, hence the species name. Photo by R. D. Bartlett.

t.f.h.

Distributed in the UNITED STATES to the Pet Trade by T.F.H. Publications, Inc., One T.F.H. Plaza, Neptune City, NJ 07753; distributed in the UNITED STATES to the Bookstore and Library Trade by National Book Network, Inc. 4720 Boston Way, Lanham MD 20706; in CANADA to the Pet Trade by H & L Pet Supplies Inc., 27 Kingston Crescent, Kitchener, Ontario N2B 2T6; Rolf C. Hagen Ltd., 3225 Sartelon Street, Montreal 382 Quebec; in CANADA to the Book Trade by Macmillan of Canada (A Division of Canada Publishing Corporation), 164 Commander Boulevard, Agincourt, Ontario M1S 3C7; in the United Kingdom by T.F.H. Publications, PO Box 15, Waterlooville PO7 6BQ; in AUSTRALIA AND THE SOUTH PACIFIC by T.F.H. (Australia), Pty. Ltd., Box 149, Brookvale 2100 N.S.W., Australia; in NEW ZEALAND by Brooklands Aquarium Ltd. 5 McGiven Drive, New Plymouth, RD1 New Zealand; in Japan by T.F.H. Publications, Japan—Jiro Tsuda, 10-12-3 Ohjidai, Sakura, Chiba 285, Japan; in SOUTH AFRICA by Multipet Pty. Ltd., P.O. Box 35347, Northway, 4065, South Africa. Published by T.F.H. Publications, Inc.

Manufactured in the United States of America by T.F.H. Publications, Inc.

Preface

Since the dawn of time, man has been fascinated by turtles. There are records going back as far as two thousand years of people keeping turtles as beloved pets. That's understandable: they are generally very small, easily manageable, and just plain cute, so in reality, this sort of benevolence is very understandable. Unlike many other members of the herptile kingdom, i.e., the snakes and the giant lizards, turtles have never wreaked much fear in the heart of humanity. In fact, as I write this, I can hear a conversation going on not more than thirty feet away between two men and a woman, and one of the men is saying, "...but generally speaking, women like turtles better than snakes," and the woman is agreeing, utilizing the theory that "...turtles are kind of nice and friendly. Snakes are so mean and...," etc. This, I think, truly illustrates the general attitude behind most people's affection for our small, shelled friends, because basically speaking, turtles are harmless. Of course there are always those that will give nasty bites, and in some cases even a little more than nasty. But for the most part, the lady is right. Turtles are harmless, and they are friendly. And that what this book is a celebration of: the wonderful world of turtles.

For most hobbyists, a turtle is more than just a pet, it's a friend. Many young children wander into pet stores, slowly slide their hands out of their parent's, and then wander off into the reptile and amphibian section, probably sensing from an early age that it's kind of "unacceptable" to keep such "icky pets," which of course only serves to heighten the appeal even further.

If the store they are in is varied enough to stock chelonians (a commonly used synonym for turtles) at all, chances are the first thing they will fall in love with is a turtle. Some of the more popular species seen on the market today are sliders (one of which, the Red-eared Slider, *Pseudemys scripta elegans*, has probably been the most popular pet turtle for the past three decades), painted turtles, map turtles, and even the occasional softshell.

Two-headedness obviously is not a common phenomenon, but with turtles it is more common than with other herptiles. Photo of a Midland Painted Turtle, *Chrysemys picta marginata*, by R. D. Bartlett.

Generally they are not very expensive (at the time I am writing this I have yet to see an expensive turtle in any pet store, and another nice point about their "economic viability," if you will, is that they are very long-lived. Children do not like to think that their pets will die someday. I'm sure if you flashed back to your own childhood you would probably remember in all-too-familiar detail how sad you felt when your dog or cat passed on. We don't wish to put anyone, particularly

our own children, through such a traumatic experience, but a turtle generally lives so long that your eight-year-old will probably be bringing it with them to college. If you can teach your young to properly care for these charming little pets, there is a better than average chance he or she will be dragging it to college! One box turtle is recorded to have lived for over 150 years! Now that's amazing. It's one thing to have a turtle as a pet, but it's another thing altogether to have a friend for life. Sounds kind of trite, but it's true.

To keep things in perspective, it must be stated that any pet, regardless of type, requires a certain degree of undeniable attention in order to survive. Whether it is something as easy as a good, hardy dog or as delicate as a tropical snake, the point is there are no true "carefree" captive animals to speak of, and turtles are no different. True, they are very tolerant of the trials and tribulations of captivity, and they also are very resistant to disease (and even when they are ill they do not show it much), but that's not the point at all.

You as a keeper have a responsibility to provide your pet with the best possible home that you can. You should settle for nothing less, because their bodies will not be able to thrive in anything less. Regardless of the fact that they live longer than most other pets, and regardless of the fact that they eat a wide variety of foods and move in a wide variety of climates, they still need all the care and attention their keepers can give them. Keep that in mind when you are making the decision as to whether or not you should keep one in the first place. Once they are in your hands, their survival is your responsibility. If they are healthy and happy, you can pat yourself on the back, but if they wither and die....

One thing I have heard many people complain

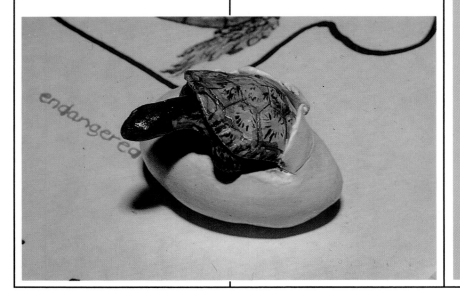

Due to the herpetological hobby's recent rise in popularity, all sorts of turtle-related artwork have begun to appear. This is a small porcelain sculpture of a hatchling Bog Turtle, *Clemmys muhlenbergii,* emerging from its egg. Photo by W. P. Mara.

Perhaps the most commonly kept turtle of all time is the Red-eared Slider, *Pseudemys scripta elegans*. The hatchling shown below is a beautiful example of what is called the "pastel" color variety. Photo by R. D. Bartlett.

about, particularly with herptiles, is that they are not true "pets" because they cannot be "petted." It goes along with the same theory that they aren't "lovable" or "affectionate" because they aren't furry, cuddly, etc. I suppose I can understand this point of view. After all, chances are pretty good no one's heart is going to melt when they see the face of a snapping turtle and compare it to that of a soft, flabby Basset Hound. But try and see it from the herpetologist's point of view. It's not just the warmth that these animals provide, it's the joy of simply being around them to study them, to learn about something unique in your world that may have

otherwise passed beyond your scrutiny. Herps of all kinds, and turtles are certainly no exception, are nature's spectres. They are the creatures that move in the shadows, unknown to all but the most educated eye. Subtlety is part of their persona, and they live up to it at every opportunity.

So to think you can hold one in your hand, to have as your very own, is really an incredible thing. I can remember in my own case, when my mother bought me my first reptile and amphibian book (I was four) and I sat paging through it, just simply fascinated at the pictures. I noticed the snakes and turtles first. What impressed me most was the

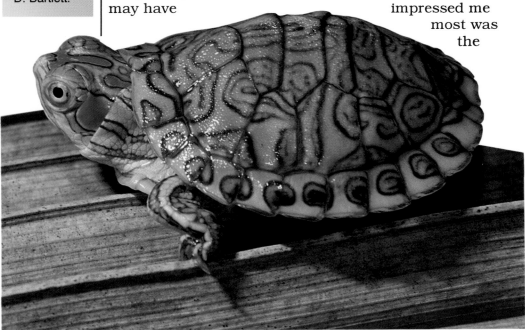

enormous degree of color variation that these animals held in their possession. One thing many people do not seem to realize is that the herptile kingdom is one of the most visually appealing on earth. I certainly noticed; it was absolutely stunning.

But then, when I got a little older, the most amazing thing happened: I found I could not only appreciate these beasts through books and magazines, but I could actually own one myself. So now, instead of being one step back by relating to a photo, I could have the genuine animal in my hand, to stare at, study, pet; anything I wanted. That, to me, was really most incredible. I was under the same impression many budding herp enthusiasts were at that very naive age: that these animals were simply part of a different world, one you could only relate to by reading about it. I was wrong, and happy for it.

So I guess the real point of this preface is not to try and convince anyone that turtles are among the world's finest pets. After all, if you're reading this now you've probably already discovered that.

No, the real point is to

simply remind you of something that you probably realized a long time ago but may have become numb to over the course of time: the immense degree of joy and elusive beauty that our good friends the turtles hold for us—all the pleasures one can enjoy from just being around them; to watch as they go through the course of their day, whether on land or in the water, and knowing that tomorrow they will still be there for us, to fascinate, to intrigue, and to enjoy.

To them, then, is this book dedicated.

Although virtually impossible to maintain in captivity, sea turtles are nevertheless graceful, attractive creatures. Photo of the Green Turtle, *Chelonia mydas*, by R. Juriet.

The Loggerhead Musk Turtle, *Sternotherus minor*, does fairly well in captivity, but it is also somewhat unpredictable in temperament and may bite freely. Photo by K. T. Nemuras.

The Basics

THE TURTLE, THE TORTOISE, AND THE TERRAPIN: WHAT'S THE DIFFERENCE?

As I go through my routines as a still-enthusiastic herpetologist, I get asked a lot of questions about certain animals. The most common one about snakes is, "Are they really slimy?" (the answer of course being an assertive 'no!'). The big frog and toad one is "Can you really get warts from touching them?" (again, no.). And one of the most perpetual about chelonians is, "What's the difference between turtles and terrapins?" or "...turtles and tortoises?" etc. Considering how important this answer will be to the rest of the book, I thought I should attend to it before covering anything else.

Speaking realistically, the main difference between the three is slight and is based on physiology more than anything else. The tortoises belong to the family Testudinidae and are purely land-dwelling creatures (the systematic name I just mentioned, and everything that goes along with systematics, will be explained later on in this chapter). Tortoises often grow much larger than other turtles and live a little longer. "Terrapin" is really nothing more than a synonym for turtle, truth be told. The word's most widely known reference is to the Diamondback Terrapin of the genus *Malaclemys*, a species

Turtles have an interesting rib cage in the sense that the ribs comprise the basic structure of the shell.

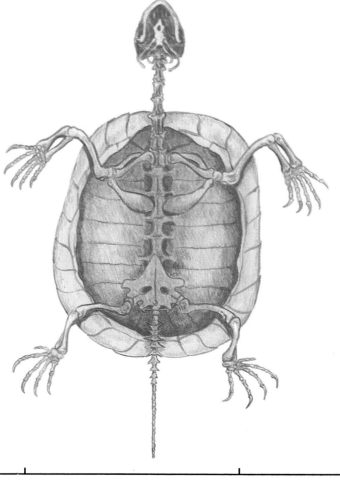

Box turtles are famous for their longevity. A specimen over 100 years old is not at all unusual. Photo of the Ornate Box Turtle, *Terrapene ornata ornata,* by Robert T. Zappalorti.

found in the eastern and Gulf regions of the United States. But the bottom line is, it's just another way of saying "turtle."

Finally, the only other members of the group that differ from the rest are of course the sea turtles. These animals are not only totally unadaptable to prolonged life on land, they are also totally unadaptable to captivity as well. In size, they're enormous (over 4 feet is not unusual), and their bodies are modified purely for an oceanic existence: instead of "feet" they have flippers, etc. They thrive only in saltwater, so if you've ever thought of keeping one, don't bother.

EVOLUTIONARY HISTORY

The evolutionary scale is an interesting thing. To think that something we see today could look totally different in another time is fascinating enough, but to also add that that time could be over five million years from now just intensifies that fascination.

Turtles have been around a long time—and that in itself is an understatement. To give you a rough idea of just how long, try this out: the early ancestors of our little friends first appeared on this earth some two hundred million years ago during a time in earth's history known as the Triassic Period, which is a parcel of time niched in a larger measurement called the Mesozoic Era. Obviously, those ancestors

did not perfectly resemble the chelonians that we know today, but they were reasonably close. The turtles we see now basically began in their present form about one hundred and fifty million years ago, and that time is called the Jurassic Period, also a part of the Mesozoic Era.

MORPHOLOGY

The turtle is certainly unique in structure; that cannot be debated. What other animal carries its home with it wherever it goes? That "home," as I have decided to call it, is known most commonly as its "shell" or, more technically speaking, its *carapace*. The carapace is made from the bones of widened ribs (on the inside) and a series of plates known as *scutes* (on the outside). The scutes are the series of clearly defined individual regions on the carapace and are very useful to the more advanced herpetologists (those who study reptiles and amphibians) for clear and concise turtle identification. Of course in the case of the sea turtles it is a little more difficult, but since there are only a limited number of those on this earth and since they are very distinct from each other, it is not a real problem anyway. Below the carapace, along the side of the turtle, is the *bridge*. This is where the carapace connects with the bottom part of the shell, which is

Some turtles have fascinating physical modifications. For example, notice the tiny worm-like appendage in the lower jaws of this Alligator Snapping Turtle, *Macroclemys temminckii*. This is used to lure prey. Photo by W. P. Mara.

Tortoises make wonderful pets, but a keeper should know that some can grow to an enormous size. The little fellow on the top is a small male Tent Tortoise, *Psammobates tentorius*, and his large friend is a Leopard Tortoise, *Geochelone pardalis*. Photo by K. H. Switak.

called the *plastron*. The plastron is also made up of a tough, bony material, and can be either very plain in appearance or occasionally very decorative, depending on the species.

If you ever get the chance to look inside a turtle's mouth, you may notice that it has no teeth. This feature is most remarkable when one considers that any turtle, regardless of size, can certainly deliver, at the very least, a most annoying bite. Their "beak" usually has a horny tip that enables them to tear their food to pieces and in fact can be quite sharp at times. Of course on some of the larger species, like the

Alligator Snapping Turtle, *Macroclemys temminckii*, for example, this can be quite dangerous for the keeper. I knew of a man who reached back into his boat to grab a net, forgot he had already caught an respectable-sized *M. temminckii* specimen that day (over 110 lbs.), and lost three fingers because of it. The point is, just because they have no teeth doesn't mean they're harmless.

A final aspect of chelonian morphology that tends to catch people's attention is their remarkably long necks. All turtles have this attribute, from sea turtles to land-dwellers. Of course, in some it is more noticeable than others. The Snake-necked Turtle, *Chelodina longicollis*, is a good example. Its neck can extend out as much as half a foot, and in extreme cases sometimes even further than that. This "advantage," if you will, is good for things like lying on the bottom of a shallow lake and quickly shooting upward to grab unsuspecting prey, not to mention the ability to curl the head around and take nips at anyone who might be picking one up when it does not wish to be handled. That is of course unfortunate for the keeper, but the turtles certainly don't mind.

UNDERWATER

One thing I am frequently asked about is whether or not aquatic turtles are *fully* aquatic, meaning basically are they able to live and function completely underwater in the same sense that fish do. I suppose if I were hard-pressed for a technical answer I would have to say no. And in saying that let me state that it is not that they can't stay underwater for long periods of time, but they can't stay underwater indefinitely. Aquatic turtles are amazing in the sense that they have two complete respiratory systems: one that involves simple air passage and return through the lungs

A turtle's growth rate will be very rapid in the wild, and even more so in captivity, as long as it is given a regular, balanced diet. Shown here are four Wood Turtles, *Clemmys insculpta*, of varying sizes. Photo by Robert T. Zappalorti.

the same way we humans do, and then a second that involves intake of water which then passes over a series of membranes and simply removes the oxygen much in the same way a fish does. But it must be understood that although this second technique is perfectly effective for certain purposes, it does not allow them to remain totally submersed for long. Considering the fact that they don't require lots and lots of air in the first place, it really isn't all that amazing to learn that they can remain underwater for a couple of hours. But sooner or later they must return to the surface and "recharge," so to speak.

AGE

One of the most appealing aspects of the turtle, depending on your point of view, is its long lifespan. Next to their unique appearance, this is probably the one thing about them people seem to remember most. In view of the facts, it certainly seems justified.

Diamondback Terrapins, *Malaclemys terrapin*, are perhaps the only turtles that are found exclusively in brackish water. Photo of a young Northern Diamondback Terrapin, *Malaclemys terrapin terrapin*, by W. P. Mara.

Example: the longest-lived box turtle, genus *Terrapene*, on record was 158 when it finally passed away! And that was only because of an accident on the part of the keeper! Who knows how much longer it would've thrived otherwise? If you think that's incredible, some tortoises are believed to have lived for over two hundred years! I don't know how true that is for sure, but the point is it's definitely possible. No one knows for certain how long any animal like this can live since even its keeper dies first. But one thing is clear: the turtles are without a doubt among the hardiest, most enduring creatures on this earth. And before we go on to another topic, let me just make one thing clear, if for no other reason than to ease the minds of anyone who thinks that if he or she acquires a pet turtle they will have to bear the burden of its care until the day they die, and even then have to pass the responsibility on to their children: for the most part, your average pet turtle will live anywhere from between ten and 35 or 40 forty years. As for how long exactly, this of course depends on the species. You probably have already realized that the land turtles will outlive the aquatics. Fifty years for the former is not at all unusual, so if you're attracted to those kinds of pets, then great.

But aquatics are not quite the same. These are the ones that you won't be carrying out to the mailbox with you when it's time to pick up that first pension check. A standard Red-eared Slider, *Pseudemys scripta elegans*, will, with the proper care of course, be around for about two or three decades. A Spotted Turtle, *Clemmys guttata*, may last as long as 20 years. And a Mississippi Map, *Graptemys kohnii*, around 15 or so. Now that's not so bad, at least for the keeper anyway. As long as it has a healthy, happy life, it doesn't really matter. Let's face it: some people just don't want the same pet for the entire course of their life. It's not

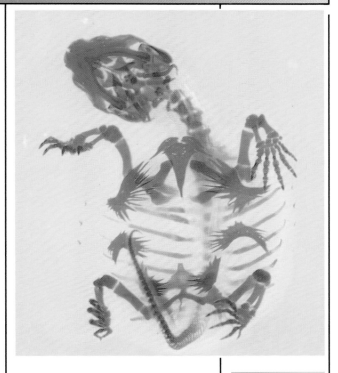

the most pleasant of thoughts, but it is true nevertheless. Naturally you can always get involved with some herp organization and simply trade in your turtle for a different one. You could also release it back into its native habitat, provided of course it was not captive-bred and raised in the first place (in which case it will be totally unaccustomed to the wild and unable to take care of itself). But the point is, if you don't want your pet anymore, don't ignore it. There are so many other better options than simply letting it wither away.

The turtle skeleton is a unique example of natural engineering. The red areas show the bones, and the blue areas denote the cartilage. This particular specimen is a Spotted Turtle, *Clemmys guttata*. Photo by Guido Dingerkus.

An albino example of a young Red-eared Slider, *Pseudemys scripta elegans*. Photo by R. D. Bartlett.

THE CLASSIFICATION SYSTEM

To finish off this chapter on the basics, I would like to take a moment out to say a few things about a subject that many young herpers, the beginners especially, seem to be almost "afraid" of due to the intimidating complexity involved. The scientific classification system that you see used in so many books, those horrifying Latin terms that might as well be written in some Martian language and make basically no sense at all, is really not all that complicated, it just requires a lot of patience to understand. To make that easier for you, let's do what the late Enrico Fermi, scientist and contributor to the development of the atom bomb, used to do with what seemed like an overwhelming problem: break it down into smaller, more manageable parts and go from there.

First, remember this: the entire idea of scientific classification centers around a series of *categories*, and within these categories are even more categories, and within those categories, etc. But again, let's break those down as well.

Today's biologists divide all animals into major groups, called *phyla*. The one we are concerned with here is the phylum

Chordata. It represents not only reptiles, but fishes, birds, mammals, and amphibians.

Now, this phylum is divided into something called a *class*, and the class our turtle friends are in is known as Reptilia. After that comes *order*, then *family*, then *genus*, then *species*, and then, occasionally, *subspecies*. It seems complicated, but it really isn't. If you take the time to look, you'll notice that only very rarely will you ever see more than just the last three categories used. For example, the Florida Cooter, a personal favorite of mine, is known in scientific circles as *Chrysemys floridana floridana*. Sometimes, if a particular animal has no subspecies, you will only see two names used, but never will it travel beyond three.

For future reference, the standard practice for spelling these names out is to capitalize everything from the genus name on up to the phylum; species and subspecies are left in lower case. If you are truly interested in learning how to master the laws and principles of taxonomic classification, please remember this: it's not as bad as it looks, just don't let it intimidate you. It takes time, but anyone can do it. At least you now know the basics.

The Bog Turtle is an example of how the classification system sometimes works. Its scientific name is *Clemmys muhlenbergii*, named after 18th century botanist Heinreich Muhlenberg, who supplied the original specimens upon which the description was based. Photo by Robert T. Zappalorti.

The False Map Turtles, *Graptemys pseudogeographica*, are so named because of the patterns on their shells, which superficially resemble those found on maps. Photo by K. T. Nemuras.

Acquiring the Turtle and Equipment

CHOOSING THE TURTLE ITSELF

First off, let's assume you've read this book so far, not to mention a few others, and have decided you're definitely going to become a turtle owner. You've thought it out carefully, you've checked the facts, and now, you're ready to take the big step.

What's first?

Well, look at it logically: the first thing you must do is decide which turtle you want. That seems easy enough, doesn't it? Wrong.

Sometimes you just won't be able to get the one you're after, for a lot of reasons. There are a few simple guidelines you're going to have to work within before you make your choice, because if you don't, you run the risk of being disappointed somewhere else along the way.

First off, you must take the time to see which ones you are allowed to have in your particular area. Many towns, states, provinces, countries, and so forth have very strict, very clear

When choosing a pet turtle, sometimes you have to make tough decisions. The Common Snapping Turtle, *Chelydra serpentina*, for example, does well in captivity but is undoubtedly unpredictable in temperament. Photo by W. P. Mara.

rules about reptile ownership. The enormous break out of salmonella disease that was attributed to turtles not too long ago played a large part in that. Check with your local environmental protection

Now that the first step has been taken, the next thing you have to concern yourself with is availability, both commercially and in the wild. But before I take that second suggestion one inch further I just want to

Painted Turtles make good pets and are still fairly abundant in their native range. Photo of the Western Painted Turtle, *Chrysemys picta belli*, by R. D. Bartlett.

agency for the correct procedures and data. They'll only be too glad to help out someone who's willing to cooperate with the law. While you're at it, try to get a copy of the list of regionally protected animals as well. After all, the information is free; you only have to pay for the phone call. Considering the potentially severe consequences, it certainly seems worth it.

say that I in no way support or encourage the practice of wild-collecting for the sole purpose of the hobby, but since it is an evil that does exist, I see no reason in pretending it doesn't. In some places it is perfectly acceptable, in others it is frowned upon. I can't say I've never done it myself, but the point is, if you must, try to do as little damage as possible. If you come across a pregnant

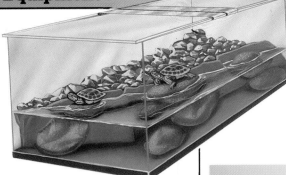

female, leave her there. If you stumble into a colony of "endangereds," let them be. In the long run it's really not worth it for either you or them.

You have to consider whether or not you can even find the specimen you want before spending the time and energy looking for it. Call around to a few reliable pet stores and see what they have. Then, run your eyes through a dependable book and see which ones are found in your area. If you're after a turtle that can only be found on the other side of the country and isn't for sale at your local pet shop, you may just have to forget about it. The only other option is professional breeders and herp societies, which can be contacted through popular magazines, journals, and newsletters.

So now that you've cut out both the turtles you can't have and the ones you can't get, the last thing you must worry about is if you are capable of giving your preferred specimens the care they will require. Although that may sound presumptuous, in essence

An adequate turtle tank need not be elaborate. A few rocks and some water will do nicely. Artwork by Scott Boldt.

If you want to go to the time and trouble, and of course if you have the land to spare, you can always provide your turtles with an outdoor pond. Photo by P. Hodgkinson.

Tanks of all shapes and sizes can be used with turtles. The taller models can be used with aquatic species to give deeper water bodies if that is what the keeper desires. Artwork by John R. Quinn.

Aquatic turtles produce relatively much waste matter that should be removed from the water in which they swim. Internal (such as the Hagen Fluval 2 model shown here) and external power filters available at pet shops are helpful in removing solid organic waste from the tank.

it is in fact a very realistic thing to consider. For example, if you think you might want a tortoise (even one of the smaller, more "manageable" species), you are simply going to need a respectable amount of room for it to roam around in. Remember, it is essential that a keeper already has a turtle or tortoise's home set up and waiting before the animal is acquired.

Along the same lines, if you don't think you will be able to give the time and attention needed to cleaning the tank of an aquatic turtle (and believe me, it takes a considerable amount of time), then perhaps you should reconsider. Even if you only

have one or two, you must still sacrifice a certain amount of your day to keep them sanitary. Think about these things, because they're all desperately important.

Now you're ready to begin choosing. On what will you base this choice? Personal preference can be a strange thing. I personally am very big on looks. If something catches my eye, it already has a good chance of ending up in my collection. At least I'll certainly look into it further. Then again, another hobbyist might want to know which ones are easiest to keep. That's the practical way of looking

at it. Perhaps certain patrons of this pastime might like the idea of basing their choices on something else entirely. Some, for example, only like to keep herps from their own area; state, province, country, etc. The point is, you really need to have a good grasp of what your priorities are. Once you've established that, you can move on. Do you like smaller animals, or larger? Patterned or plain? Terrestrial or aquatic? As soon as you've gotten all that down, then you're off and running.

ACQUIRING YOUR PET

When I initially began my involvement in the actual keeping of reptiles and amphibians, the first problem I worried myself with was, where do I get them from? Being a youngster, I had no real idea that you could simply take a trip down to the local pet store and buy one. Of course at that age not only was the cash rarely available, but just buying one wasn't half as much fun as catching one myself. Later on I learned better, but at the time I was a little more adventurous than most. What I'm trying to convey here is that you can acquire a your new pet turtle in one of two ways: you can step out into the wilderness and take your chances there, or you can go into your favorite shop and just slide the cash across the counter. In the interests of education, let's examine both.

WILD COLLECTING

Although the practice of taking herps from the wild ostensibly has declined in

The beautiful red-bellied turtles, of the genus *Pseudemys*, make superb pets. Photo of *Pseudemys rubriventris* by K. T. Nemuras.

popularity over the last few years, at least in a respectable context, follow in order to do it properly.

For one, you need to

All of the box turtles do fairly well in captivity provided they are kept outdoors, but some species and subspecies are almost impossible to obtain. Photo of six Eastern Box Turtles, *Terrapene carolina carolina*, by Robert T. Zappalorti.

serious field collecting for reptiles and amphibians is without a doubt one of the most enjoyable and satisfying aspects of this hobby. Can you really compare the thrill of spending a few hours in the wilderness and then coming across a living, breathing example of one of your favorite "herps" with anything else? Those who have done this know what I'm talking about, and those who don't may someday. But as I said before, as with anything else, there are rules and regulations you really must have to have a clear, unmistakable understanding of your local herp-collecting laws. In some places around the world, violating these laws is considered a serious offense, and the punishments can be brutal. Many conservationists the world over will argue that wild collecting for the sole purpose of the hobby is cruel, immoral, and simply outrageous. The truth of the matter is, unless you are sure the specimens you are after are reasonably abundant in the area you're planning on taking them from, it probably is best just to leave them alone. Such information about their status can be easily obtained from your local governmental agency, and should be.

Finally, if you've caught something that is sick, refuses to eat, or is undesired for whatever reason, do both you and the turtle a favor and put it back exactly where you found it. This has been a

cruel; if what you have caught falls into one of the three categories outlined above, let it go, and let it go at home.

COMMERCIAL ACQUISITION

So now that we've covered the basics of acquiring turtles in the wild, let's take a close look at the other method: buying them commercially. To most people, buying a pet is a simple procedure. Go into

Thanks to captive breeding programs, superb specimens like this beautiful Hieroglyphic River Cooter, *Pseudemys concinna hieroglyphica*, are widely available. Photo by Dr. Herbert R. Axelrod.

rule of thumb for years in herpetology. An animal that has lived its years out in a specific area of the wild is literally helpless anywhere else other than under your care. Do not be

the store, find one you like, and purchase it. That's the easiest method, but not the wisest. Pet store people are among the most unsung of all heroes, and what they do is very,

Always inspect a turtle's shell and around its eyes before making a purchase. These are the places where signs of poor health will be showing. Photo of a subadult Barbour's Map Turtle, *Graptemys barbouri*, by R. D. Bartlett.

very demanding. Imagine trying to run a business like theirs: having to manage hundreds of pieces of livestock, all in need of constant care, hoping and praying that none of them die, because when they do, it immediately pulls profits down that much further. Many of us don't appreciate this, but we should. You as the pet owner must understand that theirs is an imperfect business. Of course, if you are interested in having a new pet that will live out the course of its entire life in top condition, then naturally you are going to start with a pet store that seems "healthy." If you're not sure which ones in your area fall into this category, check around; take a few personal trips. Let your own judgment be your guide. Does the store seem

clean? Every pet store will have some degree of uncleanliness; that's to be expected whenever you have a large congestion of animals in the same place at the same time. But still, there must be a limit. Again, trust your judgment. Once you've chosen your location, ask about their refund policy. A lot of stores have one, and it's a good idea to know it. Do they take exchanges? How long is their time limit (48 hrs. is the norm, but some are up to one week)? It never hurts to ask, especially before you've bought.

So now that all that's done, the time has come to choose your pet. You know what you want, and you know where you're getting it from. You've walked into the store, found the animal in question, and have made your decision: you want to take it. What do you do now? The key words here are:

health check. No need to bring a vet along, just execute a few simple "tests."

First, study how active the animal is in its tank. Does it move around much or does it seem listless? How does it react to its tankmates, if it has any?

Next, take a close look at the eyes. Do they look swollen? Do they have any kind of opaque, pus-like covering? They shouldn't. If so, the animal might be sick. Light cases can and should be treated immediately, but more severe examples might lead you to want to reconsider.

Third, the food test. Ask the dealer for a small quantity of whatever he or she has been giving the turtle, and make sure it eats. Knowing their voracity, almost every turtle should take food around the clock, provided of course the animal is not stuffed at that particular moment. If they do not take any food they may not necessarily be sick. There are a number of reasons why a turtle may not eat, so don't be too quick in your conclusions. If a turtle seems totally disinterested in the food you have placed in front of it, try something else. Make sure you are well-educated toward what the species you are seeking is used to eating.

Many of the tortoises seen for sale these days are wild-caught. It is perhaps in the best interests of the buyer to ask whether or not the animals for sale are captive-bred specimens. Photo of *Geochelone platynota*, by R. D. Bartlett.

Sometimes it's just that simple.

Finally, just give a quick examination of the turtle to see if it has any really obvious morphological flaws. Are the limbs in good shape? Do you see any external parasites (mites, ticks, etc.)? Does the animal look thin? What kind of shape is the shell in? You don't have to be a vet to do this, just use your owncommon sense.

EQUIPMENT

Congratulations—let's assume you've gone through all the pains outlined in the last few pages and finally acquired your new turtle. You're happy with your choice, and your choice is happy with you. Is everything done now? Not quite. You still have to get some "accessories," or you might just end up keeping the animal in your bathtub! By accessories I mean tanks, lights, heaters, food, etc. It's really not a very big deal but you should have some basic understanding of the priorities of each item involved.

TANKS

The most obvious concern with a tank in respect to a turtle is of course size. If you're keeping aquatic species, then making sure the tank is absolutely watertight is also important. In today's commercial pet industry, we are spoiled in having an enormous variety of tank shapes and sizes at our disposal. For a price, anyone can have anything. Some companies even make custom tanks according to the buyer's specific wishes. This, I think, is a vital consideration, because when you are housing an animal you must give it the exact type of containment it needs. Small turtles need moderate sized homes, and large turtles need very large homes. In practice, it is simply cruel and unforgivable to place a living creature in a space where it will constantly feel cramped.

Homemade enclosures are okay in some situations (like keeping terrestrial turtles outdoors, for example), but for most species a glass is aquarium is really the best bet. After all, they can be cleaned to the point of sterility, which is of course something you can never do with wood, for example.

TOPS

Since most turtles are not escape artists

in the same spirit that other herps (especially snakes) are, there is usually no real need for a top in conjunction with an all-glass aquarium. In certain situations, like when a room seems rather dusty, you may want to place a fine screen cap on just to keep foreign particles to a minimum. It's also very important to let air circulate freely, so a totally enclosed top would be unacceptable. The one and only time you would want a top like that is if the room you're keeping your pets in is prone to drafts. Chilling an aquatic animal is a good way to kill it off quickly, and that is of course not our intention here at all.

HEATERS

Turtles, like all other reptiles, are cold-blooded, meaning, they

Hatchlings like this tiny Chinese Stripe-necked Turtle, *Ocadia sinensis*, can be kept in a simple 10-gallon aquarium during their younger years. Photo by R. D. Bartlett.

Heating is an important climatic element for all turtles. If their tanks are cold, they may begin to hibernate during times when hibernation is not necessary. Photo of a hatchling Three-toed Box Turtle, *Terrapene carolina triunguis*, by R. D. Bartlett.

are not in complete control of their own body temperature but must instead rely on the warmth around them in order to acclimate. Thus, unless you are hibernating your pets for the specific reason of breeding or to simply keep them in time with their natural biological schedules, then you must maintain a proper level of heat for them at all times. Estivation, which is a period of rest that, in nature is activated by a period of extreme dryness, is okay if the animal chooses to do it voluntarily, but if their surrounding atmosphere is a bit cooler than it's supposed to be and the turtle's metabolism is slowed to the point where it is hovering between hibernation and normal activity, there's a

very good chance it will lose its appetite during this time and simply wither away to nothing. That should give you some idea of how important correct temperature is.

If you have aquatic chelonians, your best bet would be either to invest in a fully submersible heater (which should have complete thermostatic control) or at the very least a heating pad of some sort that you can place under the tank itself to warm the water. Another option, but certainly one less favorable, is to simply heat the room in its entirety. Unfortunately this does not guarantee the water's exact temperature and also denies the animal the privilege of escaping from the heat when it wishes. As for exact temperature requirements, it is best to

simply educate yourself as to what your pet's natural requirements are, and then go from there.

LIGHTING

If we had to divide all herptiles into categories according to lighting requirements, we would have two: those that need

other periods of general exposure. This process is absolutely vital to their survival and must be replicated faithfully by all keepers. Fortunately, this is not a difficult process, thanks to the availability of a product called the full-spectrum light bulb.

Many stores carry them

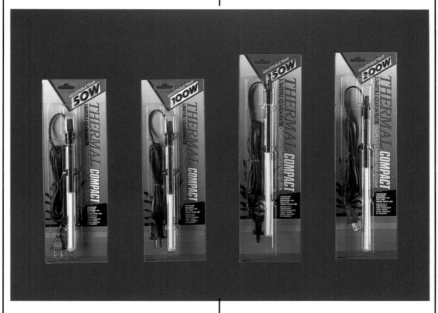

full-spectrum light, and those that don't. By full-spectrum I mean the artificial provision of what would normally be given off by the sun.

Turtles fall into the former classification. They benefit from the vitamin D3 through a process called biosynthesis, in which the sun's rays produce in the animal certain nutrients through their basking and

under various trade names. They are somewhat expensive but have a very long lifespan and make the entire process very easy, so they are unquestionably worth it. One important note to remember here though: don't let anything come between the rays of the light and the shells of the animals. Tank glass will filter out almost all of the

A reliable heater, preferably of the completely submersible type such as the Hagen submersible heaters shown here, is one of the most important pieces of equipment available to the keeper of aquatic turtles. Note that the heaters are available in different wattages for tanks of different sizes.

Captive Care

Now that you have a turtle and a place to keep it that is both comfortable and beneficial to its well-being, it's time to learn the basics of proper turtle care.

FEEDING

Generally speaking, an adult turtle should not be fed everyday, but every other day, and sometimes even less than that. Of course, turtles that come from warmer climates will feed slightly more often than those from colder ones, but for the most part it is not a good idea to feed any of them on a daily basis. It is much better to leave them a little hungry than too full.

So how much should you feed them? The answer to that is, again, not too much. You don't want to stuff them, just satisfy their appetites. A healthy, active turtle will eat until it can barely move, and that is not good. When something of this nature occurs you run the risk of giving it a variety of internal problems that will ultimately and reliably shorten its lifespan. You may have to experiment for a while until you discover just how much food is the "right" amount, but once you've

Most tortoises are good pets for keepers who don't have the patience to deal with fussy feeders. Many of them will take fruits and vegetables almost fanatically. Photo of the Indian Star Tortoise, *Geochelone elegans*, by K. T. Nemuras.

stumbled across that figure you will have no problems. Keep in mind that a turtle in captivity will not be as active as one in the wild, so the dietary requirements will already be lessened. That's a factor that many hobbyists fail to figure into their final estimations.

On a slightly similar note, keep in mind that over-feeding aquatic turtles also makes their tank water dirty much quicker, thus encouraging a whole hoard of diseases to spring up, not to mention it creates that much more work for you, the keeper.

Finally, remember that young turtles have a slightly higher metabolism rate than their elders do, so in their case feeding should occur in small quantities every single day. All baby chelonians—turtles and tortoises alike—fall under this rule. They are in their most rapid growth stage during the first three or four years of life, so nutrition is essential.

FOOD ITEMS

As I've mentioned a few times already, one of the nicest things about turtles is the fact that they accept a wide variety of food items. For the keeper, this is the best news possible because even if the pet you have is refusing to take what you're giving it at the moment, chances are that sooner or later this will not be the case. So for now, let's take a closer look at few of the more popular turtle food items to give you a better idea of what you should and will be feeding your pet in the future.

Earthworms

One of the most common food items is the earthworm. I have seen them work like magic on turtles. Many keepers who have otherwise had trouble getting their chelonian's eating cycle to "spark" into gear have sworn great success by these invertebrates. Earthworms can be found almost anywhere (if you place a piece of wet cardboard

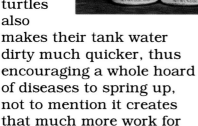

For aquatic-turtle keepers, there are many commercial products specially designed to make your feeding chores quick and easy. Photo courtesy Wardley.

Easy to store and feed, pelletized turtle foods such as the Hagen Nutrafin pellets shown here are now available at pet shops.

Crickets are perhaps the most nutritious item that a hobbyist can offer his or her turtles with any regularity. These are sold in most pet shops and can even be bred without much difficulty. Photo by Michael Gilroy.

down on some loose soil in the summertime, soon you'll have so many you won't know what to do with them all), and provide the turtle with a good, hearty meal. Of course, you should never use earthworms, or anything else for that matter, exclusively, but they're still a wonderful element.

If you're keeping your turtles active during the cold winter months remember to stock up on extra worms during the summer. Put them in the freezer wrapped individually in tin foil so they don't stick together and then simply thaw them out by soaking them in hot water for a few minutes— this must be done before feeding. Turtles can develop serious internal problems from eating previously frozen foods that have not been completely thawed. Draw from them as needed. If this is not possible, try and locate a bait shop somewhere nearby since they usually have a pretty good supply at all times. If even that fails, perhaps you can contact one of the many turtle-oriented societies and find a dealer who sells herp foods.

Crickets

Crickets are very likely the most commonly seen/bought commercial insect for the purpose of small herp feeding. Crickets are bred and sold commercially for frogs, toads, salamanders, lizards, some snakes, a variety of other little creatures, and even turtles.

In fact, crickets are probably the only truly "complete" item that a turtle could live on if it had to. Many lizard keepers swear that they have never given their stock anything else but loads and loads of crickets. Of course, every now and then they sprinkle a little vitamin powder on the crickets's backs beforehand, but for the most part crickets are indeed a well-balanced meal. They can be obtained at almost any pet store, or at the very least, again, ordered by mail through one of the many live food dealers that exist nowadays.

Mealworms
    Another food item commonly seen in many pet stores is the mealworm. The mealworm is nothing more than the larval form of a flour beetle, *Tenebrio*

molitor. For the most part, mealworms are not a very good dietary staple for most turtles and tortoises but can still be used for some nutritional purposes. For aquatic species, the mealworm will be readily consumed. Interestingly enough, it has such a violent aversion to water, most mealworms will drown eventually. But the turtles don't care; they will take them by the dozens.
    These are also very easy

Once you have gotten your turtle or tortoise eating, you may find it will begin trying different things. Photo of Hermann's Tortoise, *Testudo hermanni*, by Susan C. Miller.

Although most aquatic species have at least some carnivorous preferences, some, like this Malayan Flat-shelled Turtle, *Notochelys platynota*, are accustomed to a total fruit and vegetable diet. Photo by R. D. Bartlett.

to breed, and if given time to mature they will grow into their full adult stage.

Small Fish

For most aquatic species, treat time is fish time. Why is that? Because for some reason known only to the turtles themselves, fish are a true culinary delight. For the hobbyist who is keeping the turtle, the good news is fish are also excellent nutrition. The calcium in their skeletons is essential to a turtle's well-being and should be given whenever possible.

One tip: kill any fish first before you offer it because most aquatic species are not terribly adept at catching them themselves.

The Alligator Snapper, *Macroclemys temminckii*, has a small worm-like appendage in its mouth that seems to be specifically designed to "lure" fish their way, but this is a unique physical modification.

Fish can be purchased at your local pet store, plus a few other places as well. I myself have bought some at supermarkets just for the sake of experiment and had astounding success. But keep in mind that a freshwater turtle (and most of them are) should not be given loads and loads of salt-soaked fish on a regular basis. Try to stick

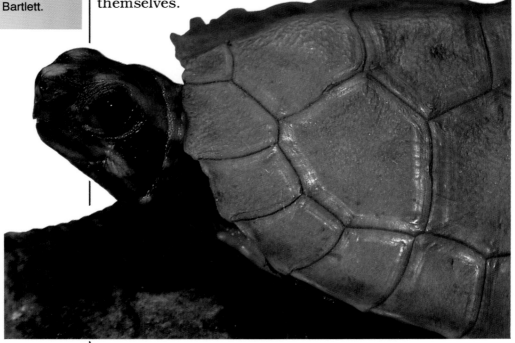

to those that are found in more fresh/brackish water surroundings, since those are the ones that their bodies will be biologically accustomed to.

Finally, just remember that although fish are a wonderful meal, they also tend to be very greasy and will dirty the tank water up shrimp (especially), and even a few others, can all be offered to your aquatic turtles without fear of crisis. The author knew a man who had three adult Northern Diamondback Terrapins, *Malaclemys terrapin terrapin*, that refused to take anything but thawed shrimp. Of

Crayfish and other crustaceans may be hard for some hobbyists to acquire, but they make great meals for turtles nevertheless. Photo of *Macro-brachium rosenbergii* by A. Kochetov.

very fast. If this is left unattended, your pet will have a filthy, grimy home in no time at all, and that of course won't do.

Crustaceans, etc.

Very briefly, I thought it might be wise to mention that many turtles love certain types of shellfish, and these are commercially available throughout most of the year. Snails, clams, course he had to soak them in vitamins every now and again since shrimp are not a complete meal, but at least the turtles were eating. However, remember again that this kind of item is basically only a "treat," and it's very easy for a turtle to get hooked just like my friend's turtles did. Be sparing in your use of crustaceans and remember that they are

Don't be afraid to steer away from traditional food items and try things that aren't mentioned in this and other turtle books. Notice the corn in this picture. Photo of Hermann's Tortoises, *Testudo hermanni*, by Susan C. Miller.

that's all you give it forever. Try anything; try everything. You'll be surprised how many different things they'll eat. I mentioned tomatoes basically because it has been my experience that they are very popular with herbivores. So are cucumbers, finely chopped spinach, and even mushrooms.

But remember, it's always good to sort of "prepare" these meals before serving. Make sure your friends aren't having too hard a time getting the meals down their throats. Try a few different things until you get some idea of what "recipe" works best for your particular animal. Then, throw it all together and chop it up until you have what might be called a "tortoise salad." Sprinkle a regular (but not excessive) supply of powdered vitamin supplement on top of it all and hand it over. That's perhaps the most wonderful thing about tortoises; once you get them eating regularly,

only an option.

Fruits and Vegetables

If you are planning on keeping a tortoise as a pet then you should know first off that they are almost exclusively herbivorous, meaning quite simply that they do not eat meat but instead sustain themselves on plants, fruits, vegetables, etc.

The best news about that is, of course, that these items are a virtual breeze to get your hands on. What's more, there's a huge choice at your disposal. If your tortoise doesn't like lettuce, try beets. If they don't like beets, try tomatoes, etc.

The key is balance. Just because your pet loves cold broccoli doesn't mean chances are they'll thrive in peak condition for the duration of their lives.

Commercial Foods

This is a strange topic, isn't it? Can you actually imagine some company somewhere that spends its time producing foods for the sole purpose of feeding turtles? It was only a short time ago that a few of the more unconscientious soup companies were making food out of turtles!

But sure enough, commercial foods for turtles and tortoises have not only carved a big niche in today's pet market, they have actually improved greatly in overall quality and are now reliable sources of chelonian nutrition.

There are two kinds: those for aquatic species and those for the land-dwellers. The type that the aquatics benefit from usually comes in small, thin, rod-like form and are comprised of a mish-mosh of vitamins, minerals, etc., that all somehow manage to actually appeal to our small friends to the point where many keepers give their pets nothing else, and they seem to do just fine. I must admit in all honesty that 90 % of these products do indeed seem perfectly adequate, so my advice to the keeper is, if you can get

Don't be surprised if some of your turtles and tortoises grab for plants and shrubs right in your own backyard! Photo of the Western Tent Tortoise, *Psammobates tentorius trimeni*, by K. H. Switak.

Newborn turtles can sometimes be fussy and difficult during feeding time. Often they will have to be offered items not usually taken by their species. Photo of a South American River Turtle, *Podocnemis expansa*, by R. D. Bartlett.

them to take it, why not? Naturally, it will always be urged that you still give your pets the occasional "treat" and vitamin supplement since creating a totally myopic diet seems so incredibly nonsensical. The hard fact of the matter is, many of these "canned" foods really do make feeding much more simple and worry-free, so how can the point be argued?

The same goes for the land-dweller foods as well. I have to confess I have not had lots and lots of experience with this, but from what I've seen it works just fine. I suppose if I were pressed for an analysis I'd have to say the bottom line is, as long as the animal in question likes how something smells, it will eat it. Thus, you can get them to eat just about anything you want as long as

they like it. This of course makes that same vitamin supplement process so much easier. It's simply a hybrid of that old "hide the pill in the peanut butter" dog and horse owner's trick, and thank goodness for it too.

Miscellaneous

There are a few other, slightly less-utilized food items that we have not yet discussed, and for a variety of reasons. For example, most people know that most colubrid snakes will take mice and rats almost anytime they're hungry. These creatures love small furry rodents, but to some that is perhaps the most disgusting aspect of the snake-keeping hobby.

However, turtles are the exact same way; at least many of the aquatic ones are.

Blanding's Turtle, *Emydoidea blandingi*, for example, will absolutely love you if you give it a nice pinkie mouse. Most *Clemmys* species

are the same way, as are snappers. The fact is, mice make an excellent meal regardless of whatever negative feelings the keeper may have about using them as a food source. The same goes with cold cuts, although meat should only be very lean and offered sparingly at best. Other unorthodox items that I have seen accepted include small frogs, chopped walnuts, hard-boiled eggs (both shelled and unshelled— land-dwellers relish hard-boiled eggs), croutons, certain breakfast cereals, bits of cheese, and bread. I even saw one turtle at a herpetological swap meet eat a wad of paper toweling. (Of course you shouldn't give your turtle paper toweling either, but it

was still most remarkable.) The point is, don't be afraid to try different things; things that have definitely identified themselves as being apart from the norm, because you just never know. As long as you think the item might be beneficial to the animal's health, what can it hurt to try it?

Vitamin Supplements, Etc.
If you've read everything else up to this point then you've probably noticed that the author is a loyal advocate of the habitual usage of vitamin supplements in the dietary life of turtles and tortoises. Why? Because they're necessary. Because your pets really can't live without them, and keeping them alive and in top shape is the ultimate goal of any good herp-keeper. Attaining that peak is a point of pride and should be stubbornly

Vitamin supplementation is an essential part of all turtle and tortoise diets. Giving your stock a respectable dose about once a month is adequate. Photo of the Red-footed Tortoise, *Geochelone carbonaria*, by Jim Merli.

Turtles that are kept indoors are often in need of vitamin supplementation. Aquatic varieties usually fall into this category. Photo of a young Mississippi Map Turtle, *Graptemys kohnii*, by K. T. Nemuras.

strived for on an everyday basis. To help achieve that goal, vitamins are a crucial consideration.

Perhaps the most important of these vitamins is calcium. Calcium is what builds the strength of a turtle's shell and promotes proper bone formation. In the wild they get this from many sources (sunlight, certain foods, etc.), but in captivity it must be provided by you, the keeper. Of course, chances are your turtle or tortoise will not take pure calcium in its store-bought form; crush a pill into powder and subtly include it with their meals.

One small problem with this that I have often heard is, if you sprinkle any kind of powder or liquid

supplement on foods for aquatic turtles, it simply runs off the moment it hits the water. That's certainly a logical and understandable complaint. Fortunately there's a simple solution too: take the item and soak it in a sealed container overnight with two things: a very light layer of liquid vitamin (just covering the bottom of the container, although make sure the food item has been "rolled" in it), and then a sprinkling of the powder on top. By the morning, the item, depending on what exactly it is, should have either soaked the mixture in to the point where it will not "bleed" enough to make any real difference or a thin paste will have formed, also giving the same desired result. For tortoises and other land-dwellers this is of course not a problem since their foods will not be offered in water.

The other major vitamin to be concerned with is vitamin D (particularly D3). This is the one that keeps your turtle or tortoise from getting a softened shell and thus becoming susceptible to a multitude of vicious diseases, even death. During the cooler season, when their metabolism is slowed, it is okay to give them occasional doses of vitamin D, provided of course you do not overdo it.

Overdoses of any vitamin can be a lot more dangerous than most people think; there have even been the occasional death stories related to such practices. Sometimes a chelonian's

system simply cannot accommodate all the nutrients that are being pumped into it and thus a severe problem results.

Generally speaking, give your pet a small quantity of calcium ("small" being relative according to the animal's size and usual meal size) about once or twice a month. You need not go crazy, just give them what you feel they need. I do not wish to make this sound like a five-alarm situation, I just want to stress that it does have to be done in some way or another. Most foods items are simply not enough, but if you take the time to give them a few extra vitamins and minerals, any concerns toward their physiological well-being will be minimal.

So now that we've gone over a few details concerning the more commonly-used food items, what else is there to know about turtle and tortoise feeding? Well, it is

A healthy-looking shell is a reliable sign that a turtle is getting all of the vitamins it needs. Notice the superb plastral quality of this Western Tent Tortoise, *Psammobates tentorius trimeni*. Photo by K. H. Switak.

Some wild-caught turtles and tortoises have difficulty adjusting to captive life. This is most apparent in adult specimens. Photo of the Helmeted Turtle, *Pelomedusa subrufa*, by K. T. Nemuras.

important for you, the keeper, to realize that turtles and tortoises in captivity are not exactly the same as turtles and tortoises in the wild. This realization should play a large part in your dietary management.

For example, in the wild, chelonians have all the room on God's earth to roam around in. A Spotted Turtle, *Clemmys guttata*, that has been taken from its two square mile lake and placed in a 20-gallon tank will not lead the exact same life it had before. Its level of activity will be greatly lessened, and thus its need for fuel will also recede.

Of course, in a situation

such as this many hobbyists like to keep their animals in good physical condition by providing them with short periods of "exercise" whereby the turtle is removed from its normal home and allowed to move about in some considerably broader territory (a swimming pool, the backyard, even the living room), and honestly, I can't say that I see anything really wrong with this (except for Aunt Martha's reaction when she drops by for a visit and sees an army of turtles scurrying under the couch).

The reality of it just might be that some of us just don't have the free time available to "walk" our turtles around everyday; and if you're one of those people, then you will have to view the matter from a different perspective.

Which brings us back to the original point: since your turtle's level of activity is less in your care than in nature, remember not to feed it as if it were going on a seven-mile hike the next day. When you overfeed, the chelonian will build up fatty deposits until it looks like a balloon stuffed with cellulite.

in this manner. I didn't realize he was eating almost all the food of the other four turtles he was housed with, and the next thing I knew he looked like a giant meatball stuffed between two clam shells. Needless to say, he was put on an immediate and vigorous diet and eventually sheared down to a respectable bulk. I certainly wouldn't let that ever happen again, and you shouldn't either, because if you do

Painted Turtles are among the most voracious feeders. Photo of an Eastern Painted Turtle, *Chrysemys picta picta,* by Robert T. Zappalorti.

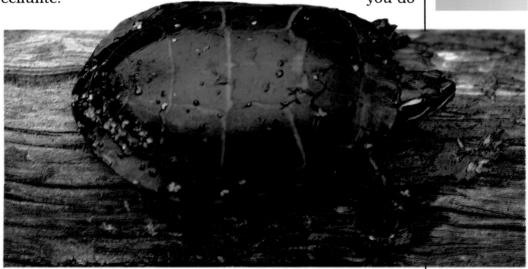

And anyone can pretty much guess what that kind of condition leads up to: a whole variety of intestinal, coronary, and lung ailments that could easily lead to death. I must confess that I once let a small male Snapping Turtle, *Chelydra serpentina*, get out of hand

you'll have nothing but problems.

Another important facet of turtle and tortoise feeding is the realization that some of them do occasionally go on little "fasts," thus driving their owners up a wall. I can remember back when I kept snakes and they

Although some of the larger turtles may go on occasional "fasts," the younger specimens, once they do start eating, will usually continue to do so all throughout their active season. Photo of a young Florida Cooter, *Pseudemys floridana floridana*, by R. D. Bartlett.

would do this for months (snakes are notorious for long fasts). For the longest time my nerves would be in tatters worrying which ones were just going to roll over one day and go stiff.

Then I realized something, and it made all the difference in the world: reptiles and amphibians are quite different from humans in the sense that when they want to, they can just simply shut down their "eating mechanism" and live off stored fats for extended parcels of time. I knew they did this when they were hibernating, but I learned later on that they sometimes do this during the active season as well.

That's when I formed this rule of thumb: get yourself a scale of some sort that measures weights slight enough for herptiles. When a turtle decides to stop eating, weigh it. After a week, weigh it again. Do this for the next couple of weeks until you have a clear answer to the question, is it losing weight or not? If not, then don't worry about it. Chances are the animal is just taking a break from eating. If you still feel unsure you can always check in with a vet, but believe me, sometimes a reptile or amphibian can go quite some time without a meal and still be just fine. I know of a snake that didn't eat for 26 months.

HOUSING

So now that you know all the basics about correct chelonian diets, the next topic to cover is proper housing and all the satellite principles that go along with it.

Tank Size

If you are planning on keeping a tortoise or other terrestrial turtle rather than an aquatic, you are going to have to accustom yourself to the unpleasant fact that these animals need a lot of room. Not so much so in the case of smaller specimens like box turtles and so forth, but then again even they will not be too happy in something like a 10-gallon aquaria.

If your tastes fall into that category, you may want to consider one of three things: either setting aside a room in your house where they can roam freely, bothering with a very large tank, or placing them outside.

First, if you have a house large enough to provide, say, your bedroom as an accommodation, then perhaps you can let your tortoise live there. A cellar or full attic will do quite nicely too, as long as they can both be heated properly.

Second, if you don't think you would mind the bother (or the expense), you can provide them with a rather large tank. This does not necessarily have to be

Housing need not be elaborate for aquatic species, and in some cases it can be remarkably simple. Here, the keeper made clever use of a clear plastic tub. Photo by W. P. Mara.

made of glass. You can actually construct one yourself out of either plexiglass or hardware cloth, etc. Since watertightness is not an issue, your freedoms are much broader. Just remember, the key here is space, and if you go out of your way to build something that large, you then need to find a place to put it.

Finally, if you have access to some land, you might want to consider housing your tortoise, etc., in an outdoor enclosure of some sort. As long as you have the proper materials and equipment, you can construct a simple "pen" for these animals with virtual ease. No advanced carpentry skills are required.

With all of these examples, you have to be sure to provide a large water bowl, a small water "pan" for bathing (tortoises and box turtles like to sit in about one inch of cool water when they got hot), a respectable degree of dry heat (since most tortoises rely on this heavily), and a secure spot to hide in. The latter can be furnished by filling a cardboard box with straw or hay and then cutting a hole large enough for them to get through in the front.

On the other hand, if you consider yourself more of an aquatic-loving type, then the problem does not become the space it self, but the size of the tank in accordance with which species you have, and how many. The general rule is, for every six-inch turtle you own, you should have about two square feet of tank space. Any less than that is basically very cruel. An adult Mississippi Map Turtle, *Graptemys kohnii*, is not going to be happy living in a 10-gallon tank, and can you blame it?

If you find yourself keeping company with a rather large platoon of chelonians, you might

want to consider surpassing glass tanks and moving on to something a bit more practical. One of those large, hard-rubber tubs used as horse troughs is a good item. Of course it may take a bit of effort to clean out (more on that later), but if you have a whole society to maintain, the choice is really already made for you.

Another good one is a baby's wading pool. These are relatively inexpensive and easy enough to find. Of course, keeping something like this indoors is

Unless you are willing to give them free run of one of the rooms in your home, tortoises and land-dwelling turtles are best kept in an outdoor pen. Photo of the Radiated Tortoise, *Geochelone radiata*, by R. D. Bartlett.

Totally submersible heaters are an excellent tool for keeping an aquatic turtle's tank water at the correct temperature. Most of them even have a built-in thermostat control. Artwork by Lisa Marie O'Connell.

always risky, but you can still either place one in a cellar that has no valuable carpeting or bury it up to ground level outside and create a lovely little "pond."

If you then take the time to enclose this area, in the summertime your aquatic turtles will be as happy as aquatic turtles can be.

Water Level

This is something a lot of amateurs seem to overlook. If you're not going to include a "basking site" for your shelled friends, then make absolutely sure the water isn't so high that they can't stick their heads out of it without pulling themselves off the bottom. Young turtles especially (which leads to the obvious conclusion that they must have a spot in which to rest on— no two ways about that)

need air. That cannot be forgotten.

Heating the Water

As I mentioned in the section on equipment, those fully submersible heaters are really your best bet, unless you honestly think one of your pets will bite through the line. I know I had that concern for a long time when I kept snappers, but apparently my worries were for naught because I never once had a problem. The best temperature to generally keep active turtles at is between 82 and 85°F (28 and 30°C).

Accessories

Any accessories that you think might "brighten up" your turtle's aquatic home can of course be added, but remember, only certain types of fake plants can be included in a wet situation safely. Overall, most of these accessories will probably get uprooted anyway. If you don't mind setting them back up all the time in the hopes of keeping the scenario more "natural," then by all means do it. Just remember to always consider the animal's safety when adding anything into the place in which they live.

Substrates

Considering the fact that everyone who keeps fish puts some kind of bedding on the bottom of their pet's tanks (usually sand, gravel, or crushed coral), most future turtle owners think they may have to do the same, since both pets are basically water-oriented.

The truth of the matter is, it doesn't really hurt to bed your turtle's tank with a light layer of stones, etc., but practically speaking, it really isn't all that great an idea either. For one, the turtles will simply move them about so much that

the attractive appearance you were going for will be immediately eradicated anyway. Plus, if you decided to keep something like a softshell turtle, you can't really run the risk of scratching their extremely delicate "shells."

Finally, the bottom line—the poor guy who has to clean the tank four times a week now has that much more work to look forward to. So as I said, it's really just a matter of personal choice, but I just gave you three good reasons why the bottom of a turtle's tank should just be left plain.

Lighting

All turtles and tortoises need something called full-spectrum lighting in order to thrive. Without proper lighting the vitamins (especially D3) cannot be properly utilized. The proper bulbs needed to achieve this effect can be easily obtained at any herp-oriented pet shop and should in no way be obstructed when in use. The rays should hit the

Regardless of where it originated, a tortoise can survive well enough on a substrate of ordinary soil. Photo of the Northern Tent Tortoise, *Psammobates tentorius verroxii*, by K. H. Switak.

turtles directly (meaning you can place them 10 feet above if you want, but don't let anything get in their way) and be in use for about six to eight hours a day. Any longer than that and you run the risk of damaging your pet's vision in the long run.

CLEANING

Now that we've gone over details about the actual housings themselves, let's talk about the final husbandry concern: proper sanitary maintenance.

For those of you who keep anything that spends most of its time on land, you are somewhat fortunate. Most tortoises and box turtles are not terribly messy. Sure, they have their moments, but they're still not half as bad as aquatics.

In the case of tortoises being outside, you should spend a few moments each week "turning over" and then compacting the soil in their immediate area so as to discourage potential health hazards. If they are inside, you must take the time to line the floor with some sort of disposable covering.

In a tank, it must be dealt with much in the same way it would be otherwise: clean all the accessories and dispose of the substrate. Wash the container out thoroughly, and put everything back in.

With aquatics, it's also basically simple; but the problem is you have to do it that much more often. It's not very nice to say, but aquatic turtles are probably the most demanding herptiles, cleanliness-wise, in existence. I have seen many a keeper literally go slowly insane, myself included, by the repetitious procedure of cleaning out a turtle's tank, filling it back up with clear, clean water, replacing the occupants, and then coming back five minutes later to find they've dirtied it again! It seems so deliberate you'd almost think they do it on purpose.

However, that is one of the many problems with being the owner of an aquatic turtle and can lead to many hours of cleaning, scrubbing, and filling. Of course, if you really don't mind then it's no big deal, but it is probably best to let you know what to expect beforehand so when the time comes you aren't too shocked or disappointed.

Here's the simplest method. You may have to translate the instructions given so they relate to your particular situation:

1) Take all turtles out of

the tank and place them in a separate container. They should all be washed with lukewarm water and a sponge (no soap or equivalent of any kind) so that any fungal buildup, etc., can be removed.

2) Remove all accessories that are not disposable (plastic plants, rocks, etc.), place them also in a separate container, and wash thoroughly using a mild cleanser at best. Rinse them very thoroughly as well.

3) Finally, remove the dirtied water by either lugging the tank outside where it can be dumped safely, or get yourself one of those small pumps used to remove water from pool covers. I recommend the latter, if for no other reason than simply for convenience. It makes matters so much easier in the long run.

Breeding

Captive breeding is one of the more positive aspects of today's herpetological hobby. It provides the enthusiasts with grade-A specimens while doing no harm to the wild.

One of the most popular aspects of the hobby of herpetology, which has become so over the last two decades, is the practice of captive breeding. In essence, this is a wonderful thing, because the way the environment is being abused at the moment, there's a better than average chance that many of the herps you see in the wild now may end up exclusive to captivity tomorrow.

If you have decided you

know enough about turtle and tortoise husbandry to consider yourself a little bit more than a beginner, and feel you're ready to take the next step and actually try breeding, then the information outlined in the following chapter should be of enormous help and interest to you.

THE BASIC PROCESS

Turtles and tortoises breed through a biological process called copulation. Through

this, the male's sperm fertilizes the female's eggs, which will then be laid in various natural locations where they will hatch some time later, producing newborn young, or neonates.

For all chelonian species, the time of year in which they mate depends largely on their geographical location. Those that live farther north, for instance, will breed in the spring and summer months when the temperature is warmer. Those in the extreme south do not have to worry about such things and therefore their schedules are radically different. The rule of thumb is obvious: the farther north you go, the later in the year the herptiles breed.

Along with that comes the interesting process of hibernation. Hibernation is a biological function performed by colder-climate species in which their bodies go into a state of enforced rest, triggered by the oncoming cold season, during which time

If a keeper is willing to learn how to captive-breed his or her chelonian stock, the reward will be a group of beautiful newborns like the Radiated Tortoise, *Geochelone radiata*, shown here. Photo by R. D. Bartlett.

Once they have begun eating regularly, newborn turtles make wonderful pets. Photo of a young Eastern Painted Turtle, *Chrysemys picta picta*, by W. P. Mara.

their reproductive mechanisms sort of "recharge" for the forthcoming active period. This process is essential to turtle and tortoise breeding because if they do not have it, they will probably not be able to reproduce. In the warmer areas, species may experience a slightly different, but still basically the same, procedure known as estivation. Estivation is like hibernation, but simply a bit milder. Those that estivate have grown accustomed to the difference, and the two are not interchangeable, so if you are planning on breeding your pets in captivity, then chances are one of

these two actions must be honored. To do this properly, a few particular steps must be taken.

Hibernating Indoors

When attempting to try this indoors, the first thing you must do is make sure the turtle(s) in question has not eaten for at least two weeks. The reason for this is because if there are any foodstuffs left in their intestinal tract while they are in the torpid state, it will ferment and eventually rot away the intestinal walls. This of course will lead to death, which is exactly what we do not want.

So what you must do is not feed them for about two weeks and then, to make absolutely sure they are "clean," give them daily warm water baths (about 80°F—27°C) for approximately two hours (only up to the neck, do not immerse them). After a week of this, they should be flushed to the point of complete safety.

Now, if the turtle you are trying to hibernate is

In order for a hatchling to break out of its shell, it must make a slit through the material. This is done with the help of an "egg tooth," which can be clearly seen on this tiny Red-eared Slider, *Pseudemys scripta elegans*. Photo by William B. Allen, Jr.

aquatic, all you really have to do at this point is fill a tank with fresh, clean water (at the same level you normally fill it to—and leave the basking site in place), keeping the water temperature at about 45°F (7°C), and simply place them inside without food. It is best to do this slowly, over the course of a day or two, so you don't "shock" your little friends and risk any damage. The tank should be left dark and undisturbed, and after about eight to ten weeks you can bring them slowly back into their normal environmental state.

On the other hand, if you are trying to hibernate a land-dweller, the technique is a little bit more detailed.

What you have to do with them is the same as the others in the beginning (no feeding, warm water bath for "flushing," then slowly bring them down to about 45°F—7°C), but afterwards they must be placed not underwater, but in a box filled with damp burrowing material to replicate what they would normally have outdoors. I have seen this done with both peat moss and straw/hay with perfect success. It is best to include a moderate layer (about one or two inches) of soft soil in the bottom of this box and to cover it with a fine mesh screen. Be very, careful not to let any drafts get to the turtle or tortoise, and check every week or so to make sure

It is not advisable to hibernate very young turtles under any circum-stances. They are not only too delicate, but don't really require such a period until they are old enough to breed anyway. Photo of a small Mangrove Diamondback Terrapin, *Malaclemys terrapin rhizo-phorarum*, by William B. Allen, Jr.

the material is damp enough. If it isn't, mist lightly with a water spray bottle. Again, remember not to spray too much. After two months, the chelonians in question should then be in a breeding condition.

Hibernating Outdoors

For terrestrial species, artificial hibernation outdoors is a lot simpler than it is indoors. For the aquatic species, indoors is best to begin with, so there's no real point in even discussing it; but as I said, for the land-dwellers, doing it outside is considerably easier. What you can do there is either dig a hole for them to burrow into (making sure it's big enough for them to move about freely and deep enough to escape the frost)

or construct an artificial "den" that is a tightly built box 2-feet square in a protected corner. This should be filled with, again, peat moss or the equivalent and checked regularly. Penning off this area also prevents many potential unpleasantries from occurring, i.e., curious animals, etc., and is just a good habit to practice.

After hibernation, many budding hobbyists try to get their stock to begin acting normally right away. It is important to realize that this is not only totally incongruous with how they react in nature, but slightly dangerous as well. Since we are warm-blooded human beings and obviously do not hibernate, we cannot possibly imagine what it is like for our shelled friends. However, we can makes educated guesses. Do you know how it feels to be suddenly awakened from a deep, sleep and then asked to start using any of your primary functions right away? It's painful, isn't it? To snap out of bed and try to do something with any kind of competency is much the same kind of shock we give our turtles and tortoises when we make unreasonable demands of them right out of hibernation; and they haven't been sleeping for eight hours, they've been sleeping for eight weeks!

Give them about a 5 to 10 day "recovery" period after you've brought their temperature (slowly) back to normal. Leave them to themselves, perhaps in a dimly lit area, and then try feeding them as usual. It may take a little longer for some, but if everything has gone accordingly you should have no real problems. Check their weight at this time to see how much they have lost during torpidity. Many will drop their bulk considerably, whereas others handle the rigors of hibernation quite well.

Okay, so now that your turtle or tortoise has been primed for the breeding season, what should you do next?

Offhand, I would say that would depend on what type of chelonian you are attempting to mate. Obviously it would not be a good idea to keep the males and females together until you are ready to let them copulate, but aquatics and terrestrials have different methods.

The Wood Turtle *Clemmys insculpta*, for example, breeds exclusively underwater. Since these are a rather large aquatic species, you will need plenty of tank space to breed them. Then on the other hand, a pair of box

Some species have become so endangered through habitat loss that they will probably *need* to be captive bred, or else suffer the consequence of extinction. A good example is the Bog Turtle, *Clemmys muhlenbergii*, of which a neonatal trio is shown here. Photo by Robert T. Zappalorti.

turtles will probably be just fine right in your backyard.

So the bottom line for the actual mating process itself is really dependent on the species in question. You can pretty much ascertain what you have to do by that rule, since it is unnecessary to say that whichever animal you are keeping you really should know something about.

EGG CARE

All turtles lay eggs, and all of the ones you will concern yourself with lay them on land in dug out nests. When it is time to do this, the female, whether aquatic or terrestrial, will crawl around until she finds what she feels is a suitable site (usually a quiet, isolated location with soft soil or sand), dig a hole about a 6 to 12 inches deep, lay the eggs one by one, and then cover the nest behind her.

Since you are probably not going to allow your pregnant mother outside to do this, you must provide her with something equitable. For the land-dwellers, its not so much a problem. If they are outside, bring them in, isolate them, and provide a "nesting box" filled with damp vermiculite, etc., so it can be moved, controlled, etc., by you. With aquatic turtles, however, you may have to go to the trouble of providing this type of situation somewhere where they can safely and easily climb out of their water, perform the feat, and then return. You want the

Contrary to some opinions, turtle egg care is really not very difficult. As long as a keeper is willing to take the time to make daily observations, turtle eggs should hatch out without problems. Photo of a Bog Turtle, *Clemmys muhlenbergii*, emerging from its shell, by R. D. Bartlett.

situation to be as natural as possible, because a pregnant mother reptile is a very delicate thing. Causing them too much stress by setting them in bizarre situations is simply not a good way to assure success of procreation.

Once the eggs are laid, make sure you do not turn them in any way. They must sit for the duration of the incubation process in exactly the same position they were laid in. Damp vermiculite, as I said earlier, is perfect for incubation. Make sure the eggs do not get wet, but permit yourself the luxury of spray misting the substrate when you feel it is getting too dry. Cover the eggs, etc., to retain the humidity, and keep the surrounding temperature at about 75°F (24°C) In a time period that ranges anywhere from six weeks to six months, you will have a little batch of new baby turtles to deal with.

CARING FOR THE YOUNG

Don't touch the young as soon as you see the young hatch out of their shells. They should remain in the incubation area until all the nutrients in their yolk sacs have been finished and they seem comfortable enough to venture out on their own.

Once this is done, you can try giving them their first food about three days later. Then, try them every single day. Turtles and tortoises have to be about 3 or 4 years old before you can really start cutting back on their diet. Obviously the adults don't eat as much as the newborns, relatively speaking, but that does not mean they should be overfed either. It's just that their metabolism is so much more demanding they need to eat more. Don't confuse more with "a lot."

From there, simply give your newborn friends all the normal care and attention that you would for any of your pets.

If possible, it is always best to have a trio of adult breeders (a male and two females), rather than just a pair. Photo of Malayan Snail-eating Turtles, *Malayemys subtrijuga*, by Isabelle Francais.

Sickness and Health

A common problem with many turtles, although most common in box turtles like the one shown here, is something called an overgrown mandible, which will need to be trimmed. If you are not capable of doing it yourself, let a vet take care of it. Photo by William B. Allen, Jr.

It is the ultimate goal of any turtle or tortoise keeper to always give their pets the best possible health

But first, let's see what we can do to discourage such unpleasantries in the first place.

conditions they can afford. The reason for this is obvious: accidents and diseases are the most feared and dreaded enemies hobbyists can deal with.

In this chapter we will examine a few of the basic concepts surrounding chelonian health. It must be pointed out beforehand that although physiological perfection is the natural goal of all conscientious keepers, the sad truth is that sometimes these things occur, and in that event, it is best to be prepared.

PREVENTIVE MEASURES

When you take on the responsibility of owning a turtle or a tortoise, you then accept every task that would normally be either theirs or Mother Nature's in the wild. You must provide them with food, water, shelter, warmth, sunlight, and clean surroundings, and all of these elements play an enormous role in the prevention of disease.

A dirty tank, for example, is a great place for fungal growth to begin. This can lead to a whole variety of external, and in the more extreme cases internal, ailments that may not even be detectable until it's too late. Of course in the case of some of the older specimens, fungal growth should not be such a cause for concern; but in the developing young it should be eradicated immediately.

Along the same lines, lack of proper lighting can do serious harm to a turtle or tortoise's bone development. The by-product of this type of illness is severe softening of the shell, which can of course lead to poor growth through a lack of calcium deposits.

In essence, the best preventive measure you can take is simple good husbandry. Design a schedule for yourself and stick to it. Keep a chart on the wall (large desk calendars are perfect for this) and be sure to record any notable developments. Or, if this is easier, keep a small pocket tape recorder handy, with a separate tape for each pet. When something happens that you feel is worth noting, simply click it on and speak your mind. One last method, and probably the most common, is to just keep a journal. But as I said before, design a schedule that encompasses cleaning, feedings, etc., and stick to it. Once you have figured out the best procedure for your

Softshell turtles are particularly susceptible to health problems. Brushing against abrasive rocks in a tank, for example, can do much damage to their shells, which of course can lead to infections and further problems. Photo of a Spiny Softshell, *Trionyx spinifera*, by Jim Merli.

particular situation, use it to your, and their, advantage. It might take a bit of time and discipline, but just think of the results. Remember the bottom line: the key to preventing sickness is simply good husbandry.

COMMON AILMENTS

One of the more unpleasant realities in the keeping of any animal is the fact that sometimes, regardless of how hard we try, a few of them just might get sick.

If you suspect one of your chelonians to be in this way, the first thing you must do is quarantine it. The reason for this is obvious: to avoid the risk of infecting any other specimens it may be

housed with. Keep the "patient" in a tank similar to the one it was previously in, so as not to shock their already depleted condition with the rigors of trying to adapt to a new climate.

Below is a brief listing of some of the more common turtle and tortoise illnesses, with comments on possible causes and suggested treatments. You can refer to this section in the hopes of possibly identifying what the animal is suffering from, thus taking the next step toward its cure. However, it should be pointed out that I do not at all encourage the practice of even the most basic veterinary measures in

Keep a close watch on your turtles's eyes, especially if you have aquatic species. Dirty tank water will affect this area first. Photo of the Malayan Flat-shelled Turtle, *Notochelys platynota*, by R. D. Bartlett.

one's home. Anything that is obviously beyond the capabilities of the amateur should be handed immediately over to the professional, because the fact of the matter is the animal's life is what's at stake, and there is no excuse for its loss due to bogus experimentation on the part of the unqualified hobbyist.

Softening of the Shell

We have already discussed this one briefly. The normal reason for softening of a turtle's shell is simply a lack of calcium. This is usually caused by an absence of it in the food items. A reasonable cure is obvious: deliberately include a vitamin supplement in their diet. Of course you should never forget the addition of a full-spectrum light.

Salmonella

One of the most common diseases associated with turtles, salmonella is a bacterial infection usually transmitted through fecal samples. It begins when a tank is dirtied and food is included, thus getting infected in the process. It is also a disease known to be transmitted directly from reptiles to people, and is relatively easy to acquire. For the turtle, it is of course best to keep their homes clean (for

Most land turtles and tortoises like to drink, so be sure they always have a supply of fresh water. A dirty water area is frequently the origin of health problems. Photo of a Leopard Tortoise, *Geochelone pardalis*, by K. H. Switak.

tortoises, watch those water bowls), and be absolutely sure that what's going into their system is as sanitary as possible.

For those who handle the turtles, a good habit to get into is washing one's hands immediately and faithfully every time you are finished. Salmonella is especially common in the neonates of the aquatic species, and many cases of children being severely affected through them has been recorded.

Mouth Infections

More common in other reptiles, oral infections such as mouth rot appear every so often on turtles, and slightly more so in tortoises. Some of the general causes include bacteria from unclean surroundings, small cuts and abrasions in and around the mouth area becoming infected, or a lack of vitamins A & D. These infections can be easily spotted by simply examining the internal regions of the mouth, looking for any swelling, discharge, and occasional hemorrhaging. The specimen will probably not eat during this time, and may even, in some of the more advanced cases, move about with its mouth slightly open since closing it has become too painful.

One of the most effective actions is to lightly cover the area with sulfamethiazine. If the infection is more severe, you may have to actually lacerate the swelling and drain it. A lukewarm saltwater solution is good for washing out such areas, and then proceed normally.

If after basic treatment the condition persists, it is best to consult a veterinarian immediately.

be taken normally, and bizarre appearances/scents in the feces. Tanks should be cleaned thoroughly if this begins, and food sources checked. As for possible cures, an ailment like this can vary highly in specifics, and with most chelonians the condition will usually become too severe when finally discovered, so a qualified professional should be consulted immediately.

Swollen eyes are one sign of a number of ailments. In this case, the Red-eared Slider, *Pseudemys scripta elegans*, pictured is suffering from hypovita-minosis. Photo by E. Elkan.

Stomach Infections

This is not terribly common with turtles and tortoises, but cases do occur. These can be detected by a pattern of vomiting foods that would

Mites and Ticks

In many captive herptiles, this is perhaps the most frequently encountered health problem. Basically it is, is an infestation of small parasites that infect not only the captive itself, but usually the extent of its surroundings as well. For a clearer understanding of these two problems, lets investigate each one separately.

Mites are extremely small invaders that usually attack the soft sections of a turtle or tortoise in large numbers. They appear on their skin as tiny dark dots (usually black or brown) and can lead to a whole arsenal of various other ailments, both internal and external. Things to watch for in your pet's behavior are rubbing against rough objects in the cage, extraneous time spent immersing itself in water, and a general loss of appetite, either sudden or gradual. To prevent extensive mite infestation, it is best to check your pets regularly. Mites can come from a large number of sources, but the most common is by simple introduction through outside creatures. For example, if you buy or find a new turtle or tortoise with mites and are not aware of it, chances are the affliction will spread, very quickly, to your other pets. Occurrences like these are the main reason for quarantining.

However, if you do indeed end up with a mite-covered animal, the best thing you can do for it is soak it in warm water for about three hours a day until the

mites in question have vanished. Sometimes this method may bring all the offending parasites to the top of the reptile's head. In that case they can be removed by wiping them off with a damp cloth. This technique may not remove all of them, but it should take most.

With ticks, the problem is usually demoted to not so much a colony but one or two parasites. When you find a tick, take a pair of tweezers and grab the creatures as close to the skin as you possibly can. Be careful not to pull too hard, or you may break the head off, in which case it will remain in the chelonian's skin and cause further problems.

If you find your efforts to be ineffective and the tick will not unlatch itself, cover it with vaseline. This will either suffocate it, or force it to let go through fear of suffocation.

Eye Infections

Finally, one of the more common turtle and tortoise disorders is a small number of eye infections. These can be attributed to a variety of bacterial infections born out of a number of sources: dirty tanks, neglected cuts and abrasions, lack of moisture, general poor husbandry, etc.

The two most noticeable symptoms of this problem are of course swollen eyes and eyes that cannot be opened. For one reason or another, turtles are particularly sensitive to eye infections, more so than other reptiles. Making sure the areas around their eyes are always clean is very important on the part of the keeper.

If you find the animal you have has indeed acquired an optic infection, you can try a variety of antibiotic eye medications or various soft vitamin gels that are commonly seen at your local drug store. Application of these onto the infected area, and then a daily removal and replacement of the old medicines, should do the trick. If after a week or so you find this action ineffective, contact a qualified professional immediately.

In conclusion, it should be said that sadly, although occasionally, turtles and tortoises do indeed die in captivity. When this does happen, make an effort to preserve the corpse as best you can (perhaps in a jar of alcohol), and then present it to a vet or a university staff. Keep in mind that this can sometimes be costly.

Facing page: Often a newborn turtle will fall victim to "soft shell," whereby its shell does not harden, due to a lack of full-spectrum lighting and a balanced diet. This is something a keeper of such young specimens will want to check for frequently. Photo of a neonatal Eastern Chicken Turtle, *Deirochelys reticularia chrysea,* by R. D. Bartlett.

A Few Interesting Species

Reeves's Turtle, *Chinemys reevesi*, a popular Asian species, was at one time placed in the genus *Geoclemys*. Photo by Dr. Peter C. H. Pritchard.

Since we have now covered all the basics of the turtle and tortoise hobby, let's spend a few moments looking at a few of the animals themselves. This chapter is designed to give you a "sampling" of some chelonian species that you may come across in your forthcoming herpetological endeavors. Not all of the ones listed are exactly what you might call "common," but they are nevertheless fascinating and therefore worthy of our study. The format is simple: a brief paragraph or two overviewing that subject's most prominent traits, done in a basic manner, for use as a point of reference in the future.

AQUATIC SPECIES

Since these are still the slightly more popular of the two, we will begin with some of the aquatic species. For the most part they are still easier to acquire, less tedious to obtain from a legal standpoint, and generally more practical. One or two may not fall into this category, but they have been presented more for interest and intrigue than anything else.

REEVES'S TURTLE
Chinemys reevesi

Over the last 10 or 20 years, Reeves's Turtle has proven itself an excellent, reliable pet and is being seen more and more in captivity these days. It is a pretty creature, with its smooth, well-defined scutes and off-brown coloration. The head is dark and simply formed, much like that of the Wood Turtle, *Clemmys insculpta*, with a very subtle series of lines running horizontally through the eyes, mouth, and so forth. They rarely attain a length of more

of humans, but will still dive off a rock or a log if someone ventures too close.

In captivity, they are easily kept, demanding nothing more than a warm climate (75°F—24°C), a nice place to rest, clean water, and the occasional feeding of anything from fish to

One of the main reasons for Reeves's Turtle's, *Chinemys reevesi*, popularity is its remarkable ability ot adjust to captive life. Photo by Dr. Herbert R. Axelrod.

than five inches, so they are easy to manage as well. They hail from southeastern China, the Philippines, Korea, and Japan, and favor quiet, slow-moving lakes and streams over anything else. They are reasonably adaptable to the company

snails to insects to just about anything you can buy at your local pet store. Can you see now why they are so popular? What could be easier than a turtle that eats anything? On a final note, they are quite easy to breed as well.

MISSISSIPPI MAP TURTLE
Graptemys kohnii

Map turtles have pleased advanced hobbyists for years, although some have demanding requirements. Photo of a young Mississippi Map Turtle, *Graptemys kohnii*, by R. D. Bartlett.

One of the more commonly seen pet store turtles, the Mississippi Map Turtle is a very attractive little animal. The carapace can range in color anywhere from a deep olive green to a light brown. Its head is usually grayish in base coloration, but has an attractive network of thin yellow lines running from the snout to the neck, in an array of variable patterns. Probably the most outstanding feature, though, is the prominent "bug eye," which is quite notably round and very wide. The adults reach about half a foot in length (males), and just under one foot in the females.

The Mississippi Map is found most prominently in the lower-middle half of the United States, basically in and around the Mississippi River basin. It favors any large body of fresh water with thick, muddy bottoms, and plenty of thick aquatic vegetation. It also spends much of its time basking, so logs, rocks and so forth are also sought.

If you are keeping a Mississippi Map in captivity, be sure it has a temperature range not below 72°F (22°C), plenty of clean water, a respectable amount of room in which to swim (a 20-gallon tank filled about halfway per single specimen), and of course a basking spot and the correct light. It feeds basically on insects, some freshwater fishes, a few shellfish, and certain plants, but if you can wean them onto a diet of commercially sold food

reasonably common pet store species, but beginning to diminish in popularity a little due to its unpredictable nature. Many seem to arrive at hobbyist's homes already ill and beyond the point of salvation, and simply decide they will not eat anymore. It is always a good idea to examine a Mississippi before purchasing, but the good news is once you have one that eats, chances are it will thrive for quite some time. They are shy and diminutive, and have a notable need for privacy in captivity.

(which actually isn't that difficult), then by all means do so. Do not forget the occasional vitamin supplement.

As far as commercial stature goes, the Mississippi Map Turtle is a

BLANDING'S TURTLE
Emydoidea blandingii

A rarely seen captive pet, Blanding's Turtle is one of the most underrated of all chelonian pets. It is attractive, hardy, and friendly.

The reason we do not see the superb Blanding's Turtle, *Emydoidea blandingii*, in captivity more often is because it is becoming rarer and rarer in the wild. In most states it is native to, it is listed as a protected species. Photo by W. P. Mara.

In spite of popular hearsay, Diamondback Terrapins, genus *Malaclemys*, are not difficult to keep. However, you may have to start them on a diet of raw fish. Photo of the Ornate Diamondback Terrapin, *Malaclemys terrapin macrospilota*, by Jim Merli.

Perhaps the most outstanding visual feature of Blanding's Turtle (at least in the adults) is the remarkable shell pattern—a dark brown base heavily peppered with tiny yellow "teardrop" spots. Of course the colors I mentioned can vary slightly, but for the most part, this is what they look like. Their heads are also distinctive, in the sense that they possess a "fish face" more so than other North American aquatic species do. Their mouths are quite wide and very powerful.

In the wild, Blanding's can only be found in and around the Great Lakes region of the United States and Canada. It is still fairly abundant in its native territory, and favors ponds, shallow lakes, and slow-moving streams with soft bottoms and plenty of thick aquatic vegetation. It will spend some time on land when basking in the sun, but for the most part it remains in the water.

When keeping them in captivity, it is best to provide Blanding's with a warm, comfortable atmosphere, but remember not to overheat them since they are used to a slightly cooler climate. A basking site is necessary but will probably not be used much. They will take almost anything you give them for food, but remember your own priorities as well. Although Blanding's Turtle loves fish, a regular diet of that will inevitably cause more work for you than you are likely to approve of. Get them started on a diet of commercial turtle food, and then supplement with crickets and the occasional vitamin mixture.

DIAMONDBACK TERRAPIN
Malaclemys terrapin

Not too often seen in the pet stores but still very interesting, Diamondback Terrapins would make fine pets if kept more often. They consist of seven different North American subspecies, ranging all

along the eastern and southern coast, and are known most prominently for their haunting of brackish water.

The Diamondback Terrapin gets its name from the notably thick, sculptured diamond shapes on its carapace. The colors vary from light gray to green to some browns or a dark black, while their heads are usually much lighter. Some have dusky white necks and heads, with a random series of darker dots all about. They are very attractive.

One of the most unique traits of this species is its dedication to brackish water settings. If you travel along the proper coastal regions of the U.S., you are bound to come across a colony of Diamondbacks sooner or later. They prefer lagoons and tidal flats as close to the actual ocean as possible. Occasionally one may turn up in a bay somewhere, but for the most part they avoid the deeper waters for something a little calmer.

If you would like to keep one of these in captivity you don't really have to worry about the light salt content all that much. I have seen many a keeper ignore this completely and go right to freshwater.

Indeed, they do seem to thrive just as well under this condition, but I would not advise it for any wild-caught adults that have grown so accustomed to the opposite for so long. They feed primarily on the obvious: various fishes (including most shellfish), but can, in time, be encouraged to take commercial turtle foods if you have the time and patience.

These are also the turtles that were so prized for their meat in the early 20th century, and more than once became the central ingredient to a variety of popular soups.

SPINY SOFTSHELL TURTLE
Trionyx spiniferus

Through the course of time the softshell turtles have earned quite a nasty reputation; and quite frankly, it is somewhat well-deserved. For the most part, softshells can be somewhat temperamental and will very probably bite whenever they can. Fortunately, some do indeed calm down after a time and in the end make first-rate pets.

The Spiny Softshell is one of those turtles. I have kept many of them and find them to be wonderfully rewarding captives. They are not only interesting to look at, they are also very practical as well.

Obviously, the most outstanding feature of the genus *Trionyx* is its remarkable carapace, coupled with its unique head. The body seems flat as a pancake, as many eastern half of the United States. They patronize a wide variety of habitats, ranging from quiet isolated ponds to fast-moving creeks and rivers. The key lies in the soft substrates, because any others will damage their delicate shells.

When keeping these in

At first, an Eastern Spiny Softshell, *Trionyx spiniferus spiniferus*, will probably object to captivity, but in time it will calm down. Photo by K. T. Nemuras.

have said, and the head has a long, thin, pig-like snout. Some eastern varieties are a beautiful coffee-with-milk tan color, and have a small arsenal of slightly darker spots in the middle. The head is also this color and the eyes are small, but round and very striking.

In the wild, they can be found over much of the captivity, always remember to provide them with some degree of privacy and don't house them with too many other turtles, especially those that could easily do them any damage (snappers, maps, etc.). Of course, it would not be a good idea to fill the tank with too many abrasive surfaces (rocks, etc.) either. They need about 72°F

(22°C) air temperature (a little more in the water), and a diet of small fish, although they can be weaned on commercial foods over the course of time.

This is a commonly seen pet store species and still reasonably abundant in the wild.

list under Appendix I (meaning basically that hobbyists simply cannot obtain one).

It is also one of the world's smallest turtles, never growing beyond four and a half inches, with a dark brown shell, dark brown head, and distinctive patch of bright

Perhaps the rarest of all North American turtles, the Bog Turtle, *Clemmys muhlenbergii*, was at one time a popular and reliable captive pet. Photo of a hatchling by R. D. Bartlett.

BOG TURTLE
Clemmys muhlenbergii

If there were one species you could probably depend on never seeing in the pet stores, it would be this one. The Bog Turtle, sometimes referred to as Muhlenberg's Turtle, is fast becoming one of the rarest species in all of North America. In fact, as of this writing, it has just recently been placed on the CITES threatened and endangered

orange right behind the eyes (this can also be yellow or reddish, but not often).

It is only found in certain isolated areas of the eastern United States (certain specific locales in five or six states), and prefers to reside in quiet, marsh-type areas (slow-moving, muddy-bottomed streams). Sunlit seepages and wet meadows are also sought, but many of these

Even if you took the time to raise an Alligator Snapping Turtle, *Macroclemys temminckii,* from birth, by the time it reached its full adult size (over 75 lbs. in most cases), it would simply be too dangerous to keep. Photo by R. D. Bartlett.

places are fast becoming extinct, and thus the Bog Turtle is too. If you find you are lucky enough to own one legally, it is best to house the Bog Turtle in a shallow, warm-water tank, with a basking site that has some soft burrowing material in it. Keep the humidity at a respectable level, and feed the animal insects, small crustaceans or shellfish, and maybe some earthworms. Commercial food can be given eventually, but a varied, well-balanced diet is essential to their delicate systems, so vitamins are in order as well.

ALLIGATOR SNAPPING TURTLE
Macroclemys temmenckii

Although I don't think it would be such a good idea to encourage the practice of keeping most snapping turtles, it might still be a good idea to educate the reader toward one specific member of that group.

The Alligator Snapping Turtle is one of the largest, and probably most vicious, freshwater turtles in the world. It can be easily identified by its pointy scutes, tan to brown carapace, and, most interestingly, the small worm-like appendage that lies in its lower jaw. The jaw is also quite unique, because it appears to be more of a "beak" than anything else. This "beak" should never be underestimated for its incredible cutting power; the adults grow to well over 100 pounds, and I personally know of people who are now missing fingers thanks to ugly encounters with one of these monsters.

They are found over much of the eastern half of North America, in deep rivers, large lakes, and occasionally brackish water estuaries. They spend very little time on land (only the nesting females will make such an appearance), but are actually reasonably placid if left alone.

They will subsist on a diet of fish, and the truth of the matter is, this is probably more economical in the long run than most commercial foods, but in reality there's a very good chance they'll take whatever you give them. They are also very long-lived too. If you manage to acquire a hatchling, plan on having it around for at least 35 years.

SPOTTED TURTLE
Clemmys guttata

One of the prettiest and most enjoyable of all aquatic pet turtles is without a doubt the Spotted. It is not only an incredibly beautiful animal, but also does remarkably

Quickly declining in wild numbers, the Spotted Turtle, *Clemmys guttata*, was at one time a popular and often-seen pet. By the turn of the century it will very likely be protected everywhere it occurs. Photo by Jim Merli.

Like its other genus-mates, the Wood Turtle, *Clemmys insculpta*, makes an excellent pet yet is fast becoming very scarce. Photo of a juvenile by K. T. Nemuras.

well in a domestic setting and actually seems quite comfortable in the company of humans.

They can be easily recognized by their dark-colored carapace (usually a very deep blue or black), and, of course, the battery of spots that give them their name. These spots also invade the head and neck region, and are usually some shade of yellow, but have also been known in red, orange, and brown.

They are known only to the eastern coast of the United States, stretching as far north as Maine and as far south as Florida, then tapering off at the top about a thousand miles inland all the way over to certain parts of Illinois, Michigan, and Wisconsin. They prefer to inhabit quiet, marshy streams, wet woodlands, and most damp meadows, and are primarily active during the early spring months.

Keeping them in captivity is a breeze. A 20-gallon tank for every two you own, with about three inches of warm (72°F— 22°C) water, a nice spot to rest on (they like to bask), and of course the proper lighting, and they will ask no more. They are good eaters, taking a wide variety of small fishes, earthworms, and insects, but will also adapt themselves to the rewards of manmade foods, so give them that as well.

Finally, the Spotted Turtle is starting to become somewhat rare in the wild, so captive breeding is something you may want to consider. They seem very willing to cooperate with such things and should be encouraged to do so at every opportunity.

WOOD TURTLE
Clemmys insculpta

Another member of the *Clemmys* genus, the Wood Turtle is known for its attractive shell and relatively high intelligence.

They can be identified by their brown, highly-sculpted, pyramid-scuted shell, dark head, and orange-colored limbs, and grow to a respectable size (almost 10 inches). The intelligence factor is derived from the fact that many of them have actually been put through series of "tests" (mazes, etc.) and proven to have the same learning skills as many small mammals. They are native only to the northeastern corner of the United States and most notably seem just as at home on land as they do in water. In fact, many herpetologists insist the Wood Turtle is the only species that seems to be perfectly balanced between terrestrial and aquatic living. They prefer damper surroundings near farms, swamps, and meadows, but are also excellent swimmers and do spend a considerable amount of time doing this.

If you wish to keep a Wood Turtle in captivity, chances are you are going to either have to house it outside with a large, sunken swimming area, or in a very big tank with a decent-sized basking site. It feeds on a very large variety of foods, including insects, earthworms, small fish, certain berries, and even some types of canned dog food, so keeping them healthy is not a problem, but keep in mind that the Wood Turtle is protected in many places and should be cared for with the utmost attention. Their populations are beginning to dwindle in the wild.

During the 60's and 70's, Red-eared Sliders, *Pseudemys scripta elegans*, were so popular, it would be safe to say hundreds of thousands of them were sold. Photo by Isabelle Francais.

RED-EARED SLIDER
Pseudemys scripta elegans

Possibly the most popular pet turtle of all time, the Red-eared Slider deserves its reputation and is an excellent captive. They are of course most noted for the outstanding mark of red that lies right behind their eyes (even in the young this is most obvious), but they also have beautifully patterned brilliant green shells with a wide variety of darker lines all along the scutes.

In the wild, the Red-eared is native basically only to the Mississippi Valley from Illinois all the way down to the Gulf of Mexico, and favors a wide variety of specific habitats. Everything from small ponds to busy river beds, but usually more in the line of anything that has a soft,

undemanding. First, you will need a fairly good-sized tank for the adults (a 20-gallon for each one at least), with about five inches of warm (72°F—22°C) water, and of course a large basking site. Change the water often, as they are a bit "messy," and be sure to provide ample lighting and humidity. Their diet is somewhat varied, which is always good news, taking everything from a selection of insects to tadpoles,

The Red-eared Slider, *Pseudemys scripta elegans*, is not the only subspecies in its species with a "red ear." The turtle in this photo is known as the Venezuelan Slider, *Pseudemys scripta chichiriviche.* Photo by R. D. Bartlett.

muddy bottom and plenty of thick plants.

If you would like to keep a Red-eared in your home, the requirements are actually quite

shellfish, crayfish, and even the occasional bits of red meat; but they can of course be just as easily trained on commercially produced foods, and when

supplemented with some vitamins and the occasional "treat," they will keep going for the entire course of their lives, which, incidentally, should be about 30 years.

TERRESTRIAL SPECIES

For the second part of this chapter, let's take a look at a few of the land-dwelling chelonians, mostly tortoises, from around the world. As I write this, I can't help but recall how very few hobbyists seriously kept these wonderful animals a mere decade or so ago. Now, thanks to the efforts of so many dedicated "herpers" who strived to obtain more and more husbandry information, tortoises and other terrestrial turtles have become just as popular as aquatics; and soon, perhaps even a little bit more.

HERMANN'S TORTOISE
Testudo hermanni

Still one of the most popular tortoises, Hermann's Tortoise can be instantly recognized by its slightly domed carapace, sculpted, shiny finish, and black on straw yellow coloration. Most of the

An omnivorous species, Hermann's Tortoise, *Testudo hermanni*, still remains as one of the most popular of all pet tortoises. And rightly so; they are excellent captives. Photo by B. Kahl.

All North American tortoises are highly protected. Photo of the Gopher Tortoise, *Gopherus polyphemus*, by Robert T. Zappalorti.

extremities are green or yellow, and the plastron of the male is only slightly, but still noticeably, concave. It is a native of many lands, including Greece, Syria, Bulgaria, Albania, and southern Hungary, and thrives in a habitat consisting of drier, more arid surroundings. If

variety of fruits and vegetables along with the occasional sprinkling of vitamin supplements.

TEXAS TORTOISE
Gopherus berlandieri

A very attractive species, Berlandier's Tortoise is an interesting-looking animal with its high-domed shell,

you wish to keep one of these, you'd better give it some space. An outdoor enclosure is strongly urged. It is best to keep a close watch on the humidity level as well. They like a nice, secure hiding spot, a good-sized water bowl, perhaps a shallow wading area, and can be fed a

concentric grooves, and brown/tan coloration. It looks very much like its close relative the Gopher Tortoise, *Gopherus polyphemus*, in many ways, particularly in the sense that both are bulky animals with short, stumpy legs. An average adult will only grow about eight inches in length, but their mass seems disproportionate. Their legs are also somewhat comical in appearance, looking more like short, flat stumps than actual limbs.

A rare species, it can only be found in certain parts of lower Texas, and spills into the uppermost tip of Mexico. It prefers mesquite ranges and scrub woodlands, and spends much of its time burrowing into the earth, which is one reason why their front legs are formed the way they are—not so much for appearance as for digging.

If you think you would like to try keeping them in captivity, you will have to provide them with a very dry climate. If the area you live in is not suitable, then this must be artificially produced indoors. They will very much want a hiding area, but since they like to burrow, it would be more logical to give them a separate area with some soft material than something like a hidebox. Of course, proper lighting is also necessary, as is a small water bowl. They will take a variety of grasses and cacti, but there are a few commercial foods that have been known to work. Unfortunately, there are not a lot of cases of hobbyists keeping the Texas Tortoise alive for very long, therefore they are not recommended as pets.

EASTERN BOX TURTLE
Terrapene carolina

One of the most common box turtles in the United

Eastern Box Turtles, *Terrapene carolina*, make wonderful, very long-lived pets, but adults will object to being kept in tanks. Photo by Jim Merli.

Notice the red eye(s) on this Eastern Box Turtle, *Terrapene carolina*. This is an easy way to tell it is a male; the female's eyes are more brownish. Photo by Robert T. Zappalorti.

Radiated Tortoises are still, fortunately, reasonably abundant over most of their natural territory. In many villages it is an unwritten rule that they be treated with great care and respect. Photo by R. D. Bartlett.

States, the Eastern Box Turtle is noted for its distinctive high-domed carapace and variable color patterns. The colors can range from yellow to orange to red, with a dark brown base. The patterning varies so much from specimen to specimen, it would be impossible to describe a "typical" model. And the interesting thing about their shells is the fact that when they feel threatened they can close themselves into it completely. Most other turtles can only partially withdraw their heads and limbs, but the box turtles turn into miniature tanks.

In the wild they can be found almost anywhere in eastern North America, and favor damp wooded areas. They will almost never stray far from water, because although they are not what one might call "aquatic," they do enjoy a refreshing "bath" every now and again.

If you would like to try

keeping one in captivity, the best thing to do is make sure they have plenty of room. These are probably the best small outdoor-dwelling species available. Many will not take to indoor situations very well, and some may not eat at all. I knew of a man who kept three in a large indoor pen, and none would eat. Frustrated, he finally put them outside, and sure enough, a day later, all three were as voracious as pigs.

Their preferred diet is actually quite varied, ranging from berries and vegetables (they are primarily herbivores) to earthworms and hard-boiled eggs (unshelled). Of course, the standard powdered vitamin supplement is also necessary, but the bottom line is, once you get them eating, you might find they take just about anything! One final note, they are among the most long-lived of all chelonians; one was recorded over 150 years old! If you manage to acquire a hatchling, plan on willing it off to your children!

RADIATED TORTOISE
Geochelone radiata

Fast becoming one of the more popular tortoise species, the Radiated Tortoise is known for its beautifully designed high-domed shell. Each scute is

A neonatal Radiated Tortoise, *Geocehlone radiata*. This species has been bred many times in captivity, and getting them to do so is not a difficult venture. Photo by R. D. Bartlett.

Leopard Tortoises, *Geochelone pardalis*, are an African species, and thus need a reasonably warm, dry environment. Photos by (top) Guido Dingerkus and (bottom) Frank Broderick.

shaped like a small pyramid and colored with a network of "sunray" lines (usually whitish yellow) on a darker base, usually medium to dark brown. The plastron is also very attractive, boasting a neat, asymmetric angular design. Adults rarely grow over 16 inches. Found only in certain parts of southern Madagascar, it favors drier, more arid regions: brushlands, sandy regions, areas with thorns, etc. It does not appreciate severe heat, but avoids dampness as well, although it needs to stay reasonably close to water for the obvious reasons.

If you decide you want to try keeping one in captivity, you are going to have to provide it with ample space to roam. This more or less rules out any type of indoor domain, and it is also important to remember its natural climate. Dryness is essential. A cool, quiet hiding space will also be appreciated. Furnish a small water bowl as well as a very shallow wading pool (no more than an inch deep) in the event that they do get too hot.

Their diet consists mostly of various types of fruits and vegetables. When they are caught in the wild, some specimens emit a high-pitched squeal, but this trait soon vanishes and does not return.

LEOPARD TORTOISE
Geochelone pardalis

One of the newest "pet" species, the Leopard Tortoise is noted for its attractive appearance above all else. The shell is like that of many tortoises, high-domed, and has a beautiful bone or straw yellow base color blotched by various shades of darker grassy plains, and savannahs. It will avoid extreme heat, but prefers dryness over moisture.

If you would like to try keeping a Leopard Tortoise in captivity, be sure you give it plenty of room to roam around in, and lots of the same dryness they are accustomed to. Since they are somewhat large, indoor

Leopard Tortoises, *Geochelone pardalis*, should be given as much room to roam as the keeper can afford. Photo by Jim Merli.

yellow, brown, and black. As adults, they rarely grow over two feet.

Primarily an African species, it is known from parts of Ethiopia, the Sudan, Tanzania, and Botswana, plus a few other African countries. It likes to roam about in dry woodland-type areas, including scrublands, accommodations are probably out of the question, so in your outdoor enclosure be sure to provide them with a good-sized water bowl and occasionally flood the earth with a garden hose so they can trounce about and cool down if they wish. Also, they like to take refuge in dense vegetation, so

A hatchling example of the African Spurred Tortoise, *Geochelone sulcata*, a close relative of the Leopard Tortoise that occurs in northern Africa. Photo by R. D. Bartlett.

providing a few thick bushes for cover might not be a bad idea.

As for diet, they will take various vegetables and, to a lesser extent, some fruit, but in the wild they eat dry grasses, prickly pear cactus, and alfalfa hay.

Leopard Tortoises are quite easy to breed, but their importation limits are becoming stricter as their popularity grows. They are still fairly abundant in their native land, but as we have learned in the past, that status could change drastically in very little time.

It is unfortunate that we could not illustrate the virtues of more terrestrial species, but since it seems their commercial availability grows smaller and smaller every year, it would not be fair to go around lauding them as supreme pets and thus lead you to believe they are waiting for you at your corner store right now. Unfortunately, due to man's environmental destructive tendencies, more and more bans are being put on their keeping, and thus a wonderful corner of our fine hobby is being eradicated.

Hopefully though, through the efforts of books like this one, perhaps that attitude will one day be what gets wiped out, instead of the animals themselves.

Suggested Reading

TFH has produced more books on the care of turtles than any other publisher in the world. You can find them in pet shops the world over.

H-1102
830 pages, Over 1800 illustrations

TU-013
64 pages, Over 50 full-color photos

H-1011
896 pages, over 350 illustrations

PS-307
128 pages, Over 25 full-color photos

KW-031
96 pages, over 95 full-color photos & artwork

Index

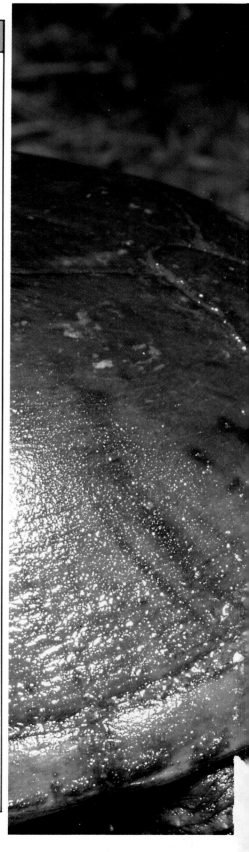